PRAISE FOR *FEARLESS SUCCESS*

"Leading a company through change is one of the most difficult challenges a CEO can face. In *Fearless Success*, John has outlined an approach that can help any leader succeed in that challenge."

—JAMES DRUMMOND, CEO of Berendsen PLC

"John's approach to High Performance is so applicable in the world of professional sports and business. This is how the best get better."

—TOM PENN, president/co-owner of Los Angeles Football Club, MLS

"*Fearless Success* will show you how to go beyond, to break all the expectations you have for yourself, and blast off into the stratosphere."

—JERRY M. LINENGER, US astronaut/*Mir* cosmonaut

"John Foley is the master at helping you achieve the highest levels of performance. *Fearless Success* is a must-read for leaders at all levels who seek to win, grow, and soar."

—JOSH LINKNER, five-time tech entrepreneur,
New York Times best-selling author, venture capitalist

"I know John, and John knows trust, period."

—DAVID HORSAGER, CEO of Trust Edge Leadership Institute,
best-selling author, *The Trust Edge*

"*Fearless Success* asks the question, 'Once you reach the top, how do you stay there?' Elite performance is deliberate, actionable, and repeatable."

—LUC ROBITAILLE, president of LA Kings, National Hockey League

"John Foley flew his way to an understanding of human potential that is as rare as the Blue Angels themselves. Fortunately for the rest of us, he has an equally rare gift for sharing that truth—in clear, compelling, and human terms. Having John as your wingman will take you places you didn't know you could go."

—GREG WELLS PHD, author, *The Ripple Effect*

"John is a living example of fearless leadership. He successfully works with the best organizations and leaders, elevating their performance by sharing technology and a proactive mindset. His wisdom contributes massive growth personally and throughout organizations."

—IAN LOPATIN, cofounder and CEO of Spiritual Gangster

"I have invested in more than 120 start-ups in my 30-year career as a technology investor, and I am now an entrepreneur myself, and yet, I am still learning about entrepreneurship from John."

—PHILLIPE CASES, venture capitalist; CEO of Readwrite Labs

"John is a fireball! His passion is real, and his messages are timeless. See him speak. Read his book. Absorb his messages. And prepare for liftoff."

—NEIL PASRICHA, TED speaker and author, *The Happiness Equation* and *The Book of Awesome*

"Hands down, the only business book I've read in years. John's message has a profoundness and truth you can touch. And it's gonna take you Beyond. Everything."

—PATRICK D. COWDEN, founder of Beyond Leadership

"The heart and soul of great companies are rooted in a culture of excellence; John has given us a roadmap. A must-read for executives."

—DICK STRONG, Chief Investment Officer of Baraboo Growth, LLC

"I've worked with a lot of speakers over the years, and no one delivers an impactful, meaningful message to clients of all types like John does. His message hits the head and the heart!"

—RICH GIBBONS, president of SpeakInc Speakers Bureau

"Since the days when John was my wingman, I have been continually amazed at his climb to heights above the clouds. In this book, he provides blue-sky clarity and a flight path to levels of performance few thought they could attain. An afterburner climb to success!"

—GREG WOOLDRIDGE, three-time leader of the Blue Angels

"John is a proven leader, and an expert in the *how* of high performance. This book will unlock a new level of leadership in anyone."

—JOHN RYAN, president of Brookfield Residential Northern California

"John Foley is the speaker that audiences are still talking about years later. His incredible energy, and his models of leadership, culture, and high performance are beyond unique."

—JON REEDE, senior partner of Rave Speakers Bureau

BEYOND HIGH PERFORMANCE

FEARLESS SUCCESS

JOHN FOLEY

CenterPoint

PUBLISHING

Published by CenterPoint Publishing
Sun Valley, ID
www.johnfoleyinc.com

Distributed by Greenleaf Book Group

For ordering information or special discounts for bulk purchases, please
contact Greenleaf Book Group at PO Box 91869,
Austin, TX 78709, 512.891.6100.

The cover picture is the author's personal helmet. Blue Angels® and TOPGUN™
are protected marks of the Department of the Navy. Depictions of the Blue
Angels® are used in this publication with authorization of the Naval Aviation
Trademark Program Office. Neither the Department of the Navy nor any other
component of the Department of Defense (DoD) has approved, endorsed, or
authorized this publication. The views presented are those of the author and do
not necessarily represent the views of DoD or
its components.

Glad To Be Here®, CenterPoint®, and Diamond Performance®
are registered trademarks of John Foley CenterPoint Companies, Inc.
High Performance Zone™ is a trademark of John Foley CenterPoint
Companies, Inc.

Design and composition by Greenleaf Book Group
Cover design by Greenleaf Book Group
Cover image of jets ©David Gaylor. Used under license
from Shutterstock.com

Publisher's Cataloging-in-Publication data is available.

Print ISBN: 978-0-692-12989-0

eBook ISBN: 978-0-692-15306-2

Part of the Tree Neutral® program, which offsets the number of trees
consumed in the production and printing of this book by taking proactive
steps, such as planting trees in direct proportion to the number of trees
used: www.treeneutral.com

Printed in the United States of America on acid-free paper

19 20 21 22 23 24   10 9 8 7 6 5 4 3 2 1

First Edition

CONTENTS

Introduction 1

CHAPTER 1 **High Performance:**
How the Best Get Better 7

CHAPTER 2 **Beliefs:**
Activating Your Highest Potential 23

CHAPTER 3 **Dynamic Focus:**
Sharpening Your Mind 55

CHAPTER 4 **The Brief:**
Connect, Align, Commit 77

CHAPTER 5 **CenterPoint:**
The Power of Purpose 99

CHAPTER 6 **High Trust:**
The Key to Execution 119

CHAPTER 7 **Culture:**
Connection and Extension 135

CHAPTER 8 **Glad To Be Here Debrief:**
Secret Sauce 151

CHAPTER 9 **Beyond High Performance:**
Glad To Be Here 171

Acknowledgments 187
About John Foley Inc. 189
The Glad To Be Here Foundation 191
About the Author 193

Introduction

*"What began as a pursuit of aviation mastery
eventually became the pursuit of mastery itself."*

—John Foley

Great teams and true masters of their abilities are extremely rare. This is a book about how those individuals and teams think, act, and achieve lives filled with extraordinary results. On this journey, we'll examine the culture and the cadence that elite teams use to achieve excellence and sustain it under constant change. We'll uncover the fundamental processes and the clear mindset needed to ignite extreme high performance. And finally, we'll examine how the best of the best see things differently, and how that vision changes the world around them, allowing them to create their own destiny. The destination is a place where beliefs, focus, trust, accountability, and gratitude converge to create a sacred space that few have experienced, but which is accessible to anyone who has a thirst for improvement.

Along the way I'll share some stories from my personal experience of elite performance. From my time landing fighter jets on aircraft carriers, to my time as the lead solo pilot of the US Navy's Blue Angels, I was allowed the honor of representing the US Navy. I learned to push my mind, my body, and one of man's greatest flying machines—the F-18—to the absolute limits of their potential. The Blue Angels are widely considered the world's premier flight demonstration squadron. Being a part of that team was the experience of a lifetime, but it was only the beginning of my journey into high performance. What began as a pursuit of aviation mastery eventually became the pursuit of mastery itself.

As you might expect, flying with the Blues had a profound effect on me. But what you might not expect is—even more than the rarity of the flying we did—it was the experience of an elite culture of excellence and gratefulness that has had the most profound impact on my life. Becoming a Blue was a challenge in itself, and once I got there, I had to elevate my performance beyond what I thought was possible. When I realized I had the potential to achieve continuous, incremental improvement, as well as exponential shifts in thought and execution, it changed the way I understood success forever.

The destination is a place where beliefs, focus, trust, accountability, and gratitude converge to create a sacred space that few have experienced, but which is accessible to anyone who has a thirst for improvement.

I'm thankful for what I achieved as a pilot, but the ensuing journey has given me wisdom about the nature of our capacity to succeed and improve. In fact, being a pilot with the Blue Angels was only three years of my life. Later on, I was accepted as a Sloan Fellow at the Stanford Graduate School of Business. Following that, I had the opportunity to compete in the world of venture capital during the boom and the bust of the dot-com bubble. Gaining an understanding of how successful businesses and people operated—both what worked and what didn't—inspired me to take everything I'd learned as a member of an elite organization and redefine it in the context of business results.

These days, I work with some of the world's top organizations and leaders, helping them understand the mindset and processes that enable higher performance. I've been refining these concepts for decades, working to break down my unique experience of excellence and create concepts that are easily actionable. To date I've helped more than a thousand companies make complex ideas simple and repeatable.

Lean startups, Fortune 500 companies, and world champion athletes all have something in common: a thirst for improvement that inspires them to reach the very tip of the pyramid. The approach throughout this book is based on techniques that the greatest teams and organizations use, and that I personally depended on in extreme situations when my life depended on precise execution. I'm going to show you how to make the complex simple, meaningful, and scalable—something that enlightened leaders know and do all the time. Each time you pick up this book, it will be like climbing into the cockpit of a Blue Angel F-18. As the canopy closes and we prepare for takeoff, I hope you feel anticipation and excitement. My genuine desire is that you and your teams will elevate your expectations and achieve your greatest dreams.

I'm going to show you how to make the complex simple, meaningful, and scalable— something that enlightened leaders know and do all the time.

As much as it thrilled me to wear that gold helmet and blue flight suit of a Blue Angel, the thing that still captivates me today is the idea that any person, any team, and any organization can achieve higher and higher levels of performance. And I'm not just talking about more money, bigger bottom lines, and more success. I'm also talking about the place beyond high performance that is only measured inside each individual soul. Some call it life purpose, others call it personal mastery. It inspires us to reach for the horizon beyond the horizon and enter the realm of the unseen that lies beyond our expectations. That is where our path here will eventually lead.

I've seen the impact this journey can have. I've seen it in the eyes of people from all corners of the globe, across all industries, in men and women alike. I've met people after a speaking engagement who cannot wait to get home and share these ideas with their children and families. I've had people open up and share their deepest struggles and their greatest dreams, grateful for the impact and the inspiration this experience provided them. It has the power to spark a total change in your life by reigniting something already inside of you, energizing a passion and thirst for something greater than yourself that will drive every action you take, every day of your life.

Through this book I will be taking you on a ride that will challenge the way you live. My hope is that this journey will transform the way you think about business and interact with your teams. I want to ignite purpose and passion in you, your relationships, and a greater good.

It's time to strap in and take it to a whole new level.

"Burners, ready! Now!"

Mastery inspires us to reach for the horizon, beyond the horizon, and enter the realm of the unseen that lies beyond our expectations.

1

High Performance:
How the Best Get Better

*"Only those who will risk going too far can
possibly find out how far one can go."*

—T. S. Eliot

"Ready, HIT IT!" I bark into the radio, 1/10 of a second before
the blue streak of another Angel crosses over my canopy at
1000 mph closure. I feel a thump from the airflow as the two
jets' shockwaves collide. We've just passed each other within
a wingspan.

I'm flying 80 feet above the tarmac, moving so fast I'm cov-
ering two football fields within the span of a heartbeat. Well,
maybe the span of a normal heartbeat. But this isn't normal; this
is right in the middle of one of the world's most awe-inspiring
air shows. When you're inside that cockpit, extreme focus,

preparation, and execution have a tangible effect on reality. Everything appears to slow down as your mind speeds up.

I call on the radio, "Gucci's clear," and my wingman responds, "Thumper's clear." (Gucci is my call sign.) Simultaneously, we slam the sticks back toward our guts, propelling the nose of the aircraft up into the clear blue sky, using the full 32,000 lbs of thrust generated by the F-18's afterburners. I'm pulling 7.2 G's without a G-suit, using my strength and training to bear down and squeeze my entire body—legs, arms, gut, face—grunting, straining to counter the force of gravity that's trying to drain the blood from my brain.

"Standby . . . ROLL!" I execute a 180-degree roll. I'm upside down now—still climbing at 400 knots. As I look back over my shoulder, I can see the crowd on the ground 1,000 feet below. To them, the scream of the engines gets quieter as our jets shoot upward into the sky in graceful synchronization. I call again, "Standby . . . ROLL!" bringing my aircraft back to level before I call on the radio, "Gucci's clear." My wingman responds, "Thumper's clear." Now I take another 7.2 G max deflection pull, as I alert the Boss and the diamond pilots we've finished our maneuver. The flight line is clear as we get in position for the next sequence.

You've just experienced 16 seconds in the cockpit of Blue Angel #5, the lead solo pilot of the Navy's Flight Demonstration Squadron. This is what it's like when my wingman and I execute the "Knife-Edge Pass," one of 30 maneuvers we will perform during an air show.

When you think of the Blue Angels, what comes to mind? Your first thoughts are probably words like *awe, inspiration,* or *excitement.* When you peel back to the next layer, you start to notice things like precision, excellence, and teamwork. Those are all true of the team, but the appeal and the power of the Blues are not limited to impressive aerial maneuvers. The team is also defined by more subtle attributes like commitment, focus, trust, and consistency. Those are the qualities that set us apart and make Blue Angel high performance unique and applicable beyond the bounds of the air show. Learning how we performed at the highest level and how we activated those qualities in the team can open your mind to new possibilities in yourself and in your team, the same as it did for me in those air shows.

Just how elite is this Blue Angel team? To put it in perspective: more than 4,000 climbers have reached the summit of Mount Everest; there are currently 2,450 active Navy SEALs; the world has seen 536 astronauts travel to outer space; and the Roman Catholic Church recently selected its 266th pope. But since our inception in 1946, there have been only 257 demonstration pilots who have flown as Blue Angels. In other words, only 0.01% of all US military pilots in history have worn the gold helmet.

During training you learn right away why so few people have done it. It's not your typical nine-to-five job. Heck, it's not typical in any regard. The standard of excellence is set to the utmost level. Yet we do it every year. Seventeen officers and 110 maintenance troops carry on a tradition, continuously refining, adapting, and raising the bar.

One major challenge of flying an air show is that mistakes have a high consequence. But once when a journalist asked me if the flying we did was dangerous, I instinctively said no, that what we did wasn't dangerous, just *inherently unforgiving*. That idea planted a seed that came to fruition years later when I started to ask myself why I felt that way.

It's pretty unique to feel safe when your job is to strap into a seat attached to two massive jet engines and go screaming through the sky, through cities, over water, upside down, with the belly of another jet bucking in your face an arm's length away. Granted, there is *some* element of that experience that my personality finds naturally exciting, and maybe you do, too; but in the moment, you don't have time to think about having fun. If you listen to the tapes of my cockpit mic when I was flying, you can hear the intensity vibrating. We're talking full-on body grunts that make you sound like a wild animal, digging your heels into the last ounce of your strength conditioning to clench every muscle in your body, fighting as hard as you can against the force of 7.2 G's. That much G-force makes it feel like a massive weight is crushing every inch of your body. It amplifies the force of gravity by 7.2 times, meaning that if you weigh 170 lbs like I did, under that much G-force you now weigh 1,224 lbs! All the while, you have to keep the jet on a precise razor's-edge flight path. When you transition out of the maneuver, it's at the exact millisecond that you've practiced thousands of times. When you come back on the radio, it's with a calm voice. "Gucci's clear."

Even knowing the danger, having experienced it moments before the interview with that journalist, the reason my mind made that distinction was that I knew something they didn't.

I knew the rigors that we had all gone through before the air show that very day and in the months preceding. I knew the challenges we'd all been through in our careers as naval aviators. There were hard lessons, some learned in blood and others in the mind. We all knew the Cats and Traps[1] of countless carrier takeoffs and landings, straining the eyes to find the pitching deck in the dead of night while dark, icy waters lay in wait, beckoning for a momentary lapse in concentration.

Those shared experiences formed the basis of extreme trust that the team shared. It was innate in each of us. The team dynamics were a necessary element for navigating an inherently unforgiving environment. That's true of the greater world, too. Think of the countless startups and brilliant entrepreneurs for whom success can hinge on the smallest advantage: something like a thought, an instinct, or a simple belief that they can persevere. Think of the massive global corporations struggling to align thousands of moving parts and people, trying to adapt and lead through the speed and change of this century. If you zoom out, the world that surrounds us every day is no less extreme than the environment inside a Blue Angel air show.

Our trust in one another wasn't the only thing that allowed us to perform in extreme conditions. We also had a deep trust in the system that got us there. That system, a process and a mindset that we engaged with every single day, was designed with continuous improvement in mind. It outlined the way that we practiced and executed, and how we got prepared before every flight. It influenced all of our behaviors, both in the cockpit and

---

1   Cats, or catapults, are used for launching jets off carriers, while traps refer to the arresting wires that stop jets when they land on the carrier deck.

in our lives generally. It allowed the team to get better month after month, day after day, even as personnel changed.

The Blues face a unique challenge that makes our process and our approach especially important. Throughout the Navy, all personnel are reassigned to a new unit every three years. For the Blue Angels, this turnover includes the maintenance crew as well as the leadership, so the structure and traditions of the team are a huge priority. Can you imagine walking into your job each year on New Year's Day to see that roughly a third of your colleagues and half of the leadership are brand new? That kind of change and growth can cause disruption if your culture and systems are not designed to handle them. In a high-performance organization, individual talents will come and go; but the culture and the process of the organization need to be so strong that change doesn't negatively impact forward motion.

For the Blue Angel demonstration pilots, the turnover is even faster. Pilots usually serve only two years, which means half the demo team is new every year. The faster transition for pilots comes from three main factors. First, the honor of serving as a Blue is something we want to share with other qualified candidates, because there are other naval aviators who have the skill to take on that precision flying and the character to adopt a purpose larger than self. That was our biggest mission, actually—to serve as the Navy's ambassadors of goodwill. It was our mission to inspire awe and dreams in people around the world, and we did it not only with air shows, but also by serving as examples of honor, courage, and commitment.

The second reason the turnover rate for Blue Angel pilots is so high relates to the stress and pace of a show season. Each year, we spend over 270 days away from home, and go more than 300 days without having two days off in a row. That kind of intensity is taxing for your body, your mind, and especially your family.

The third reason might not seem obvious: it's the risk of complacency. We all know that getting too comfortable can lead to distractions, whether it's in business or in relationships. Over time, that can lead to severe consequences. When you're flying in formation an arm's length from another jet, you need to do everything you can to make sure you are laser-focused and that complacency doesn't set in.

Establishing a process that you can trust and that everyone buys into is one of the key goals of this book—but there are two sides of the coin. The best of the best combine strong process with a distinct mindset. That's what differentiates elite performers. Your mindset defines the way you think. The way you think defines your behaviors. Your behaviors drive execution, which creates results. A mindset of caring will elevate every thought and outcome. As you'll learn, the core mindset that is woven throughout this book is embodied in a simple phrase: "Glad To Be Here." Those four words can actually change the way that you perceive the world, unlocking the potential that brings exponential results.

This combination of process and mindset is the key to activating high performance in yourself and your team. Throughout the book, I'll be sharing elements of both.

"Glad To Be Here." Those four words can actually change the way that you perceive the world, unlocking the potential that brings exponential results.

THE MINDSET: GLAD TO BE HERE®

I call the ethos that runs through this book the *Glad To Be Here Mindset*. This mental approach is the real game-changer. It's at the core of why high performers do what we do. This larger purpose gives us the energy to overcome even the most challenging obstacles. It's the key to resiliency. It bonds the individuals of great teams, and it lies at the heart of exceptional organizations. Glad To Be Here is the differentiator, the one thing that takes these excellent processes and inspires breakthrough results.

If you take only one thing from this book, let it be these four words. They imbue every action with a sense of purpose, possibility, and profoundness. This attitude has had the most positive impact on my life of anything I have ever experienced. I've seen it do the same in countless individuals, teams, men, women, and organizations from all walks of life in countries around the globe.

When you perceive the world through the lens of Glad To Be Here, you see things that others don't see and you have the confidence to take action. That's innovation. What one person sees as a threat, you see as opportunity. Where one person observes a struggle, you perceive just another step in the journey. Where one person feels stuck, you sense the key to transformation and innovation. This is exactly the kind of differentiator that you need if your goal is to take yourself beyond your current state. High performers see things differently.

When you perceive the world through the lens of Glad To Be Here, you see things that others don't see and you have the confidence to take action.

On the Blue Angels, we used the phrase "Glad To Be Here" at the end of our opening comments during our debriefs. These words are the sign of a culture of respect and gratitude. We all shared that purpose—from the pilots to the support crew—and it drove us to be the best we could possibly be. Our gratefulness came in part from the fact that every day we were putting ourselves in an inherently unforgiving environment, and every successful flight was something that inspired gratitude. But it also grew from the rare opportunity to serve others in one of the most thrilling and awesome ways. The Glad To Be Here mindset is more than a reaction to circumstances. When you start to understand how extreme the life of a Blue Angel pilot really is, you'll start to realize that this mindset is not the icing on the cake, but a critical foundation of the culture. In fact, it's so rooted in who we are, it helps create a purpose larger than self—to serve as ambassadors of goodwill. That higher mission is what drives us to be the best of the best.

These four words are rooted in something familiar and

accessible to every single person on this planet: gratitude. In psychological terms, gratitude is special because it requires an awareness of our personal mental state. A growing body of research has established the special role that gratitude plays in the development of relationships and results. It underlies all kinds of relations, from close bonds between friends and family to professional ties we feel with colleagues or teammates. That's why Glad To Be Here is the differentiator, the spark that ignites all of the key elements that teams are looking for, such as chemistry, trust, and camaraderie. When people actively engage with this emotion and allow it to define their being, it promotes a state of mind that allows for open and honest human interactions with more efficient outcomes. This kind of activity translates directly into business results.

In addition, studies have indicated that gratitude has a contagious and cascading effect that naturally spreads beyond the initial participants, such as the far-reaching benefits of "paying it forward" found in a joint study by UC San Diego and Harvard.[2] When you begin to see how powerful gratitude is, you sense how it actually fuels the journey into higher performance. This becomes the most important part of everything that you do. It can lead from success to significance.

For the more than half a million people in direct audiences that I've shared it with, Glad To Be Here becomes an awareness that you take with you into the world. It's a conscious awareness that imbues your life with positivity and growth. It's a state of mind that brings positive energy to yourself and those

---

2   From "'Pay It Forward' Pays Off" by Inga Kiderra, http://ucsdnews.ucsd.edu/archive/newsrel/soc/03-08ExperimentalFindings.asp, accessed April 2018.

around you. And this energy allows you to be resilient and face challenges with grit and determination.

There is a profoundness in this state of mind, which ties back to a purpose larger than self. As you continue on this journey, Glad To Be Here will become both the *how* and, more importantly, the *why* that elevates your thoughts and your actions. Put simply and boldly, Glad To Be Here can change your life and change the world.

It's one thing to feel Glad To Be Here, but it's another entirely to share it. At the core of this mindset is gratitude, which is a social emotion. When you share the Glad To Be Here mindset with others, it has benefits for you, and for the person receiving. It's not just something you keep inside to make yourself feel good or elevate your performance, it's something you share with the world around you that can have a transformative effect on your surroundings.

> *Put simply and boldly,*
> *the Glad To Be Here mindset can*
> *change your life and change the world.*

I've seen this cascading effect happen many times. I like to close certain sessions with what I call a "Glad To Be Here Share-out." One person begins and we go around the room, giving each person a voice to express why they are Glad To Be Here. The exercise is simple, but the emotion it draws out can be astounding. It only takes one person sharing a deep, heartfelt story, and the room completely transforms. It gives everyone a rush of connection and camaraderie, inspiring them to open themselves up and share themselves in the purest sense.

You may be thinking that Glad To Be Here sounds like the outcome of success and not the catalyst, but in my experience, it was an essential tool for achieving high performance. It may be easy to imagine feeling Glad To Be Here when everything is going well, like when business is booming or when victories come easily. But actually, Glad To Be Here is most important in times of trial. Reminding yourself of the sources of your gratitude is an awesome way to drive out fear and immobility. It connects you back to your higher purpose. It refocuses the mind on the positivity, allowing you to spot new opportunities for innovation and execution. It's the differentiator that can turn a bad situation into a great success.

When I fully embraced Glad To Be Here, my life was imbued with a purpose that pushed me to continually achieve. More importantly, it drove me to give back to the world, to inspire and to share with others. I found my life transformed by a positive emotion that seemed to change the way I thought about everything. And it was infectious, impacting everyone around me and elevating my surroundings.

The power to change a single person's life is also the power to change the world.

The power to change a single person's life is also the power to change the world. That's the level of importance that we should give to this mindset. Finding deep engagement with

Glad To Be Here is natural. Think of it as a tool you can call on that will boost your performance and enhance your personal success over and over again.

PROCESS: THE DIAMOND PERFORMANCE FRAMEWORK

If you want to achieve high performance, you need to pair a strong mindset with a strong process. The *Diamond Performance Framework* is a process built from fundamental concepts. In basic strategic management theory, success relies on four things: vision, plan, execution, and feedback. This methodology underlies the actions of most successful businesses and teams. Sometimes we refer to this as operational excellence. But at the most elite level, we think differently, we speak differently, we act differently, and we get different results. We take a unique approach to these fundamental concepts. When you're talking about how the best get better, small things matter.

The Diamond Performance Framework (or DPF) takes each of these fundamental concepts to the next level. We're not just going to talk about vision; I'm going to show you how to get commitment and buy-in to a vision. I'll take you beyond planning regimens and show you how to create focus and alignment for individuals and teams. When it comes to the task at hand, you're not just going to execute; rather, I'm going to show you how to leverage high trust to get the most from every action you take.

After you execute, you'll need to get feedback. And in the DPF, feedback plays a prominent role. I'm going to give you a method for debrief that not only examines what happened, but also allows you to reassess and helps to create a culture of

DIAMOND PERFORMANCE FRAMEWORK®

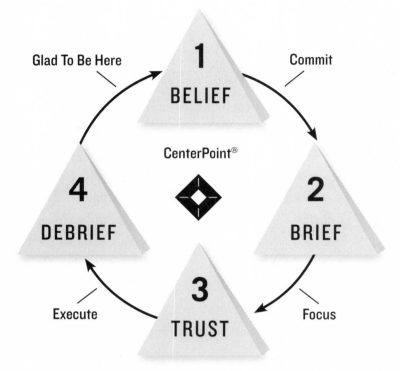

accountability that breeds personal responsibility. This inspires ownership with focused actions that reverberate throughout the organization. It's also a tool for building chemistry and trust that inspires ownership.

This process is made up of various techniques that have subtle yet significant differences. This is not meant as a replacement for your current procedures. Instead, it's an enhancement designed to be overlaid onto your present operations. It was created to work with different kinds of people, and with a variety of objectives. The goal is to take your current performance and imbue it with the edge that high-performing teams use to get ahead and stay ahead of the curve, sustaining excellence, over and over again, even through changing conditions. This approach is repeatable, it's transferable, and it works. The more you use it, the more it accelerates and spirals upward, allowing you to deal with perpetually smaller increments. As you see the increasing results, it empowers an energy that propels one to higher and higher levels, breaking belief barriers and driving exceptional performance.

ORIGINS OF THE FRAMEWORK

The DPF is more than a product of my time as a Blue Angel. When I created this system, I took the core processes we used to fly air shows and adapted them for use in business and in life. It is the combination of my rare experiences as a Blue Angel, the time I spent at Stanford business school, the lessons I learned as an entrepreneur, and the wisdom I've gained in the last two decades helping over a thousand companies reach for higher performance.

Working with other high-performance teams showed me I needed to create a framework that was repeatable in different situations, and especially in a changing environment. Just like in business, sports, or life, success is about more than achieving excellence. It's about *sustaining* excellence through change: changing markets, changing economies, changing people, and changing dynamics. The ability to adapt to change was central to what we were trying to achieve when I was a Blue Angel. But the ability to ignite and lead through change is what enables success in all aspects of life. The future favors the bold.

It's easy to tout the benefits, but how do you actually do this? How do you make this process and mindset part of your DNA, and part of your organization? How do you think and act Glad To Be Here in a genuine, positive way?

The future favors the bold.

For many of us, this has become the journey of a lifetime.

For me in particular, those four words that began as a simple phrase have now become the foundation of how I think, act, and speak—in all corners of my life. The same has been true for many of my clients over the years.

So, as we strap in, take a moment to pause and bask in this mindset. Imagine the things in your life that make you Glad To Be Here. Imagine the state of awe that people feel being in the audience at a Blue Angel air show, gazing up into the sky and seeing those powerful machines soar with grace and precision. Imagine what it would be like if people saw your performance— personally and professionally—in the same way. Imagine how it would feel if your actions and your attitude inspired awe in those around you.

That is what it means to achieve high performance, and it's only the beginning.

2

Beliefs:
Activating Your Highest Potential

"Find the place inside yourself where
nothing is impossible."

—Deepak Chopra

High performance begins with a belief. There is a concept in cognitive psychology that states that we as human beings don't perform at our full potential; rather, we perform at a belief level. It follows that if you can raise your beliefs, then your performance will follow. If you can raise the beliefs of a team or an organization, then their performance will follow those new beliefs. And if you can raise a child's belief, or quite possibly a whole society's belief, transformational change will follow.

I remember the first time I heard that concept, it made sense to me—but I wanted something more than an intellectual understanding. I needed to connect it back to direct experience. In fact, we have to ground all of these intellectual principles in reality; and that's one of the challenges of a book like this. How do you take concepts that make sense on the page and make them real in your life?

Looking back at my journey line, I can see clearly that my life was shaped by a deeply held belief that was ignited in my heart when I was 12 years old. It was the day when my dad took me to my first air show. I loved my dad; I wanted to be just like him. He was an Army officer and an engineer, and to me he was the embodiment of wisdom and integrity.

I'll never forget that day at the air show. The scream of the jet engines was deafening. There was power and precision in the sky as the planes soared together in a single welded formation. I remember the sudden exhilaration of a low-altitude, high-speed pass and the smell of smoke oil in the air. The sheer energy flowing from the jets coursed through the crowd; I could feel it charging everyone around us. In my mind it was both magical and very real. When the show finished, I turned to my dad and said, "Dad, I'm going to do that."

When I spoke those words—which, as I look back, seem pretty bold, given the odds—I felt them in the core of my heart. It hit me like a vision of the future. I had no idea how hard it would be, but through the twisting path of my life I always maintained the belief that I could achieve this goal. It was my dad who took me to the air show; but it was my mom's total faith in me that fueled my beliefs. She was always my biggest fan.

When I became a Blue Angel, they both came to as many air shows as they could. I vividly remember my mom standing in the front row waving a small American flag. She was never afraid, but always seemed to be living in a state of joy, which everyone could feel. She would join the team in the caravan on the way into the show and make friends with the police escort. Among the fans in the crowd she was always a hit. I've had so many people tell me their favorite part of the air show was watching her enjoy the experience so fully.

BELIEVE IN YOURSELF, *AND* HAVE A BACK-UP PLAN

Beliefs and faith will keep you going, but few journeys follow a straight line. If you want to maintain forward motion, you need to understand that change is constant. Especially in our accelerating world, resilience is the key to overcoming obstacles. It's one thing to have a vision—especially as a child; it's another thing to make it a reality. You have to adapt and adjust. You need to have a plan B. In fact, oftentimes for me it was even necessary to have a plan C.

In any endeavor, things may not work out exactly as you expect. Often the difference between success and failure is resilience. It's not what happens to us but how we react to it that really matters. Embrace challenges, for they build endurance, which in turn builds character; and with strong character you are ready for anything.

Often the difference between success and failure is resilience. It's not what happens to us but how we react to it that really matters.

A *belief* in your ultimate success can help you remain resilient if you suffer a setback. I speak from experience on this. Right after high school, I nearly missed the chance to become a Blue entirely. I put in my application to the Air Force Academy and received a letter back saying that I had been medically disqualified. I was confused because I was a young athlete, in great physical shape. I read further and learned the disqualification came because there was too much protein in my urine. I thought—and still think to this day—what the heck is that!? In the end, it was a good thing I got disqualified, because the Blue Angels aren't part of the Air Force, they're a Navy squadron. I had applied to the wrong team! Regardless, the medical examination is the same for both academies, so I applied right away for a reevaluation. Very quickly, I got the same rejection back. Again, what the heck was this pee thing?! Turns out it may have been the result of my trying to make weight for the wrestling team. Anyway, I couldn't be deterred. But the time to be accepted to the Academy that year was about to pass. I had a hunch my limitations could be overcome, so I put in for a medical waiver. Even though it would mean waiting a year, if I got the waiver, I would be able to enter the Academy the following year.

In the meantime, I needed to make the best of my situation and do something to keep myself moving forward, and maybe even enjoy myself for a while. Growing up, I had always loved both skiing and playing football, so I enrolled at the University of Colorado. The year I spent there proved really important for me. It gave me a chance to grow and experience life. Like any college kid, I ate lots of pizza, had lots of fun—maybe a little too much my first semester—and got to experience life at a civilian school that I would have otherwise missed.

I chose Colorado because they had one of the best college football programs at that time. I'd been a good player at a small school, but by no means was I a blue-chip recruited athlete. In fact, at 5'9" and 165 lbs, I wasn't anyone's ideal candidate. But I did have qualities that would serve me throughout my football career: tenacity, determination, and the deep belief that my abilities could help the team win.

Being a respected program, the team in Colorado was built mostly from scholarship players, but I decided I was going to make the team as a walk-on. At most football programs when you walk on, they run you hard for three days. It's a journey to hell and back in shorts and a t-shirt. They run drills until you have to quit; that's the goal.

I made it through all the drills on pure grit, but I was still worried about being cut for my size. I felt like I had to do something—anything—to make myself stand out. After the last day of drills I saw the coach on the field; I knew he would be making the recommendation that day for who got cut and who stayed. I walked right up to him and said, "Coach, just give me the pads."

There was a boldness in my request—the product of my upbringing, when I learned that anything is possible with hard work and determination. I still wonder what he saw in me that day, but whatever it was, he gave me a chance and handed me the pads. The next day I was on the scout team, working with the third- and fourth-string guys running simulations of the opposing teams' plays that the starters needed to practice against. I was small and inexperienced compared with some of the team's top talent, but playing against the best players on the team at practice every day gave me the chance to prove my worth. It also beat the snot out of me! But that's how it works in an elite program. You have to pay your dues; you have to prove your worth in front of the team.

I deeply enjoyed my time in Colorado, but I still carried that belief I had formed when I was 12, and never lost sight of my ultimate goal of flying jets. Eventually, I got the medical waiver and a letter telling me I'd been selected to join the Naval Academy in Annapolis. The career opportunity that would change my life was about to begin. I finished out my second semester at Colorado and prepared for my next move. Fortunately, my time playing football with the Buffaloes gave me experience that I used to my advantage when I played defensive back for the Navy Midshipmen. Eventually I had the opportunity to play in two bowl games and helped build one of the best four-year records in Navy history at that time. I'll never forget the moment in my final game when I intercepted a pass in the Liberty Bowl against Ohio State. I probably wouldn't have been there if it hadn't been for those years getting beaten up at the University of Colorado. The time at Colorado planted the seeds that allowed me to excel in Annapolis.

That's an important lesson that I learned over and over again. Sometimes you need a plan B, and even a plan C. But in the end, because of my belief, I got where I needed to be. The Academy gave me a shot at flying jets, but nothing was guaranteed. You have to work hard, and everything you do—academics, military bearing, even football—all plays into the decision for who gets to fly and who doesn't. To this day, I believe that extra year at Colorado—though it was unplanned—actually played to my benefit. Coming into the Academy, I had a deeper desire to buckle down and do the four years of work it would take to achieve my goal of flying jets.

LET YOUR DREAMS GUIDE YOU

Sometimes I wonder how an idea I had as a child—my dream to one day fly jets—turned out to be an unwavering guide. I think it comes back to the question: Where do dreams hit us?

Think about the last time you had a dream or deep aspiration. Where did you feel it? The key here is that dreams hit us in the heart, and not in the head. A dream is something you feel at the core of your being. But you can't function on raw emotion alone; you have to connect the dots between the heart and the head. Even though that's a distance of only about 12 inches, sometimes that's the longest journey.

> *Dreams hit us in the heart,*
> *and not in the head.*

It's the same in business and in life—a dream alone will not get you success. For that vision to become reality, you need a strategy and a plan. You need resilience and a strong willingness to adapt. But an unwavering belief in the dream or the vision often remains the most important part of what we achieve, because it plants a seed in our hearts. Your thoughts come from these kinds of seeds; your actions come from your thoughts; and results come from those actions. In this way, achievement is not possible without these initial seeds. We plant them, and then we have to water them, tend them, and help them grow. At some point, the seed will open. Sometimes we don't know when it will happen, but it must happen. In my case, it wasn't until decades later—when I finally put on the Blue Angel flight suit and gold helmet for the first time—that I realized how profound that air show with my dad really was. But I'm getting ahead of myself.

Once I got to the Naval Academy, the path toward achieving my dreams wasn't any straighter than it had been the year before when I landed in Colorado. Academically, I wasn't the best in my class; I actually fell somewhere around the middle. At the Naval Academy, every student is ranked based on academics and military bearing, and professional development. Keeping up my military requirements while playing Division 1 football and pursuing a degree in mechanical engineering proved a lot to take on. It took work, and it was a lot less fun than Colorado; but I managed to finish in the middle of my class. That was good enough to achieve my goal and get a pilot's slot. But I also learned something else. Seeing how I just barely got into that pilot's slot, I realized I needed to raise my game; being average wasn't going to work in the next phase of my life.

For basic pilot training, all candidates arrive in Pensacola, Florida, the cradle of naval aviation. It takes about two additional years to finish flight training, after four years at the Academy. At that point, you've finally earned the right to wear the Navy wings of gold. On the day of the wing-pinning ceremony, you officially become a naval aviator. But you still don't know which airplane you're going to fly.

During all pilot training, your performance is constantly evaluated. Every flight factors into your standing, and at the end, class ranking plays into who gets to specialize in which type of aircraft: jets, props, or helos.[3] The top 1/3 of the class typically chooses jets, which—since I graduated #1—is exactly what I did.

Once you have your type of aircraft, the training starts all over again. I was stationed in Beeville, Texas, for jet training, and spent another year mastering specialized fighter tactics. I started on a twin-engine jet called a T-2 Buckeye. Then I moved into advanced jet training on the A-4 Skyhawk, an attack airplane that the Blues actually flew in the 1980s.

During this phase you learn all of the difficult tasks that Navy pilots are known for, including landing on carriers, dropping ordnance, and training in air combat maneuvers. Once again, everyone is ranked, and this rank plays a big role in the final selection process. Everyone puts in their request and they go to the #1 person and assign the aircraft they will be flying, possibly for their whole career. The best pilots typically pick fighters, then attack aircraft, with the remainder going to support jets. The top-ranked pilots usually get their first choice, but there are no guarantees.

Around this time the Navy was unrolling its first F-18 squadrons, and I really wanted to get one of those assignments—everyone did. The F-18 was the peak of technological advancement. There were a lot of great airplanes in the fleet, but this was like choosing between a Ferrari and a Ford, and the F-18 was the sleek, shiny Ferrari. The problem is, pilots don't get to pick their planes. Nevertheless, there I was, a complete nugget (that's what we call rookies in the Navy), and I had my

---

3   Jet engine aircraft, propeller-driven aircraft, and helicopters.

eyes on the assignment that all the veteran pilots in the fleet were competing for.

Did I let those slim odds deter me, and steer me toward the clunky old Ford? Of course not. Are you starting to see the thread here?

SOMETIMES YOU JUST HAVE TO ASK

After flight training, I put in my request for a specific aircraft. I chose the F-18 as my first choice; but I was denied. The plane was too new, and they were only taking more experienced pilots, ones who had already flown the F-4 and the A-7.

My commanding officer (CO) called me in and told me that I had some of the best grades in the last couple of years, but there were simply no F-18 slots for young, inexperienced pilots. He said I had to pick something else.

I was dismayed, but I wasn't defeated. I wasn't going to let my lack of experience get in the way of achieving my goal to fly the F-18, and eventually, to fly for the Blue Angels. I decided to take it to the next level—a step above my CO—so I called the Pentagon. When I got through, the switchboard operator wasn't sure where to direct my call. After some back and forth, somehow I got on the line with Captain Rud, the head of aviation detailers who assigns all the pilots in the Navy. Normally, this guy would never be working to assign student pilots. He's way up the chain, dealing with who gets command of what squadron, or who's going to be a TOPGUN instructor.[4] That I was even going to talk to him was crazy.

---

4 TOPGUN™ is the popular name for the Navy Fighter Weapons School, an elite program that trains Navy fighters in air combat maneuvers.

When I finally got through, I was straight with him. "Sir, Ensign Foley here, calling from Beeville, Texas."

There was a pause on the other end of the line. I could tell he was thinking, *Why is this student pilot calling me? How did this kid get through?*

But I pushed on. "Sir, I'm calling because I just finished flight school, and I want to fly the F-18. What can I do to get into one of those squadrons?"

He paused again, and I was sure he was going to hang up. To my surprise he said, "Let me get back to you."

I don't know if it was my outright boldness at calling a superior like that, but something led to us having a pretty amazing exchange. Here was someone in an important role, taking a small moment out of their day to help someone who had passion in his voice. It's a lesson that has stuck with me, and one I share often with leaders: be generous. A small effort on your part can have a huge effect on someone else.

The captain called me back shortly and said, "There's no way I can get you the F-18 initially, but there's an A-7 Corsair squadron that I've gotten word will shortly be transitioning to the F-18. If you can make it to this A-7 squadron, you'll get the plane you're looking for quicker."

To Leaders: Be generous. A small effort on your part can have a huge effect on someone else.

I was thrilled; this was it! Here was some inside information that I could use to pursue my dreams. He also told me that in his three years of being in charge of all the pilot assignments in the Navy, I was the first student who ever called him.

Lesson learned—ask and you shall receive![5]

It was amazing news, and the next thing I knew I was in Fallon, Nevada, training to fly the A-7 with the VA-122 replacement squadron. Out there in the desert, I was working to master the skills that I would one day use to fly an air show. It's also where I experienced one of the defining moments of a fighter pilot's career: I got my call sign. Pilots use call signs for easy communication over the radio, but they also inspire camaraderie among the team. You always dream of having a cool call sign like Maverick or Iceman. But the thing about a call sign is that you don't get to pick it, it's assigned to you by your peers. Some call signs reflect a part of your personality or your physical appearance, but others, like mine, get applied after you do something stupid.

Fallon is a tiny desert outpost, and we were a small class, only three pilots (they used to call us the three stooges). One day after a flight the instructors asked the three of us to meet in the lobby of the bachelor officers' quarters so we could drive into Reno and go out for a night on the town. The training had been intense, and I was looking forward to getting out of Fallon, so I dressed up a bit with a collared shirt and a thin

---

5   It turns out our lives would intersect multiple times after that first conversation. Captain Rud later became the CO of the Blue Angels, and we met in person for the first time when I was applying for the team. At a recent reunion, we discussed our original conversation, the day the switchboard operator put me through to him. I told him how he'd impacted my life with a simple conversation and great advice.

black leather tie. Looking back, that wasn't a very cool look, even in the '80s! I walked into the lobby and saw that every one of the other pilots was wearing a t-shirt and jeans. It was obvious that I was the odd man out. One of the other pilots said, "Hey, what's with the leather tie?" and another one blurted out, "That's Gucci!" Everyone burst out laughing. Add that event to the fact that I was driving an Alfa Romeo at the time, and the combination gave my fellow pilots all the ammo they needed to assign the name. I didn't like it, so of course, it stuck. It's still with me today: Gucci!

STILL DREAMING OF JOINING THE BLUES

Through my early years in the fleet I was always focused on doing my best in my current assignment, but I never lost sight of my dream to fly with the Blues. I had several assignments in the Navy before I thought about applying for the Blue Angels. To even be considered as a Blue Angel you need to achieve a great deal as a naval aviator.

Getting there is a lot like getting somewhere in the business world, actually, because it starts by establishing a minimum competency. There are basic factors, like a minimum 1,500 flight hours and your CO's endorsement. But it doesn't stop there. You need to have flown jets off carriers and operated in the fleet on multiple deployments over a three-year period. After you've been deployed in the fleet, typically candidates for the Blues have become instructor pilots in the replacement air group or TOPGUN. But consideration isn't limited to technical skills; what they're really looking for in Blue Angels is someone who wants to be there and understands the greater mission of the team. The Blues need people who are willing to be ambassadors of goodwill and take on the task of making a difference in people's lives. While the Blues are made up of combat fighter pilots, when you join the team, your mission changes and your new focus is to inspire hopes and dreams in others. That's what it means to be an ambassador of goodwill.

Whether you're flying off carriers, dogfighting,[6] or teaching someone else how to do those things, your skill is the product of your environment. The harder the environment or the more extreme the conditions, the more you grow. Landing a jet on a carrier, for example, is extremely difficult. To put it into perspective, a typical civilian runway is around 10,000 feet long. On a Navy carrier, the landing area is about 600 feet long. You have to drop your jet within a space of 120 feet to catch one of the four arresting cables that snag your jet's tail hook and stop you violently, within a few hundred feet. The short size of the runway isn't the only challenge; this runway is also moving, both away from you and pitching up and down with the swells of the ocean. As a naval aviator, you also have to contend with extreme factors, like the pitch black of the sea at night, or bad weather, or coming back from a mission low on fuel. Situations like that start to give you a picture of what our environment made us. When you push the limits, the limits start to push back. You can feel it. You either deal with the pressure, or suffer the extreme consequences.

---

6   Dogfighting is a term that is used to describe airplanes engaged in air-to-air combat. It could be one or multiple airplanes fighting against each other. We practiced for these engagements by doing what we call ACM, or Air Combat Maneuvers.

When you push the limits, the limits start to push back.

These are the moments that increased my capacity and defined me as a person. This is what it takes to be a Blue Angel. You have to be seasoned to pull off the next-level flying required in the air show, and there's only one way to learn at this level: experience. As the expression goes, "Iron sharpens iron." That's why naval aviators are known internationally as some of the best pilots in the world: the inherently unforgiving nature of dogfighting and landing on aircraft carriers demands the most out of every pilot in the fleet.

So by the time I applied for the Blues I had achieved a fair amount of experience and accolades. I was a six-time top-ten carrier pilot—with over 300 aircraft carrier landings. I'd been a post-maintenance check-flight test pilot, and served as an instructor pilot with the Marines' most advanced fighter training squadrons, VM-FAT 101, the Sharp Shooters. I was NATOPS,[7] qualified to fly three different jets: the A-7 Corsair, F-14 Tomcat, and F/A-18 Hornet. I even got to do some of the real flying in the movie *Top Gun*. When you see those scenes on the carrier, the heat coming off the engines, the jets flying off the deck, that's my fellow air-wing pilots and me in the cockpit! Tom Cruise and Val Kilmer even spent some time in the mess hall getting to know us. I just happened to be in the right place at the right time, flying off the USS *Enterprise* when the crews came aboard to film.

---

7   Naval Air Training and Operating Procedures Standardization; provides procedures and operational specifics for all elements of US Naval Aviation.

Once you're eligible, formal application for the Blues requires the endorsement of a CO and three letters of recommendation. This had been my lifelong dream, so toward the end of my tour with the fleet, I wanted to apply. There was a slight problem, however. During that tour, my CO—who had planned to endorse me—rescinded his support when I made a major mistake. During a practice sortie, I accidentally fired a missile. Yeah, you think you've made some mistakes at work? Try lighting up a live heat-seeking missile and shooting it toward the corner office.

When it happened, we were out in the middle of the ocean. During a practice sortie, you practice both dogfighting and dropping live ordnance in the ocean. In the process of dropping ordnance, my wingman joined up on me and said, "Hey, Gucci, you got a hung bomb." A hung bomb is one that fails to drop, and you have to execute emergency procedures to jettison the ordnance before you land back on the carrier. Emergency procedures have clear checklist items, but I didn't use the checklist this time, as I thought I was in a hurry, and we were in the middle of the Indian Ocean. I messed up one of the steps—a bit of a mix-up in what we call switch-ology—and instead of dropping the ordnance, I fired an active heat-seeking missile. The good news was that my wingman was clear, and out there in the middle of the ocean, it just landed in the water. It was still a major mistake, however, and I was grounded for three days.

In the debrief that followed, I told them what had happened, and that I had not used my checklist. I was in a hurry, and I hadn't turned to it. Therefore, I had gotten two steps reversed. During that grounded period, the gravity of that situation bore down on me and I had a profound realization. Originally, I thought not using the checklist was the core issue, but in fact, that was just a material cause. The root cause was that I had gotten complacent about handling live ordnance. I realized complacency was something that could create so many different kinds of dangerous situations. I knew then it was something I needed to tackle head-on, every day. In the end, this proved to be an extremely valuable lesson.

A SECOND TRY

I had to wait a full year before the next application window opened. In that time, I had moved on to a role as an instructor pilot with a Marine fighter squadron. I worked myself out of the previous hole, reestablished myself, and built the confidence to ask my new CO to endorse me.

For my letters of recommendation, I reached out to people who deeply knew me. One was Captain Bud Orr, the CO who taught me to fly A-7s. By this time he had become a carrier air group commander with a lot of power and respect in Washington. I'll never forget what he wrote on my endorsement. He said, "John wears his heart on his sleeve. Sometimes that vulnerability can be a detractor, but for John it's not, because that's who he is and that's who you get."

With all the necessary pieces in place, I sent in my Blue Angel application. When the letter came back saying I'd been accepted for consideration, I knew there was a long road ahead. Acceptance just gets your foot in the door. Then you have to fly to the Blues and prove to them that you want to be part of the team.

I had to visit the team during my own free time, on the weekends. I requested a jet from my CO, and the next couple of weekends I flew across the country and met the Blues wherever they were performing that week. I thought it might take another year before possibly being selected because I was younger, less experienced, and had fewer flight hours than a lot of the other applicants. Still, I resolved to give it my best shot and see what happened.

After a couple of months visiting the team, I started to see what made it so special. I got to sit in on the preflight briefs, and got my first taste of the culture of excellence that would soon change the way I looked at my performance, and my life. At this point in the process, there are many pilots observing the team, and little did I know the team was observing us too. In order to choose the final candidates, the team was watching how we interacted, not only with the officers, but with all the maintenance troops and spectators as well.

Eventually, I was selected as a finalist, and I flew to Pensacola to spend quality time with the Blues in their home base. In this last meeting, you sit and face all 17 officers for a formal interview. I gathered to wait with the other candidates in the Blue Angels' "pilots' room," which is the office for the current demo pilots. It's filled with memorabilia and pictures of teams from years past. It's an incredible experience to be in the presence of this tradition and greatness.

When I got into the interview, it began with casual questions as well as conversation between all of us. Eventually, they asked a question that I wasn't quite expecting. "Gucci," one of them asked, "have you ever done anything dumb in an airplane?" I paused for a fraction of a second, and I remembered the recommendation from my CO that had gotten me the interview. I decided to lay it on the table. I said, "Are you kidding me? Multiple times." I'm not sure that was the typical answer. I went on. "One time, I almost shot down my wingman when I accidentally fired a missile."

I told them the whole story, and I could see something change in their faces when I started to talk about complacency. I told them what I had learned both from a material and root-cause standpoint. It was years later, in my third year with the team, that I would really understand how important that lesson was for becoming a Blue Angel. When you're flying in formation at 36 inches, complacency kills, not just you, but potentially your fellow pilots too. Being able to avoid complacency is one of the most valuable attributes a Blue Angel pilot or anyone else can have.

When you're flying in formation at 36 inches, complacency kills, not just you, but potentially your fellow pilots too.

I left the interview feeling unsure, but having no regrets. When I got back to the pilots' office with the other applicants, I gave them a heads-up about the "have you done anything dumb in an airplane" question. I didn't want them to be caught off guard. This openness proved meaningful months later when one of the other applicants told me it had showed him how I wanted everyone to succeed.

In the weeks that followed, I did my best to stay focused on the job at hand and not remind myself how close I had come. Finally one day, the duty officer said, "Hey, Gucci, you've got a call. Blue Angels." I leapt to my feet, found a private room, and took the call. The Boss was on the phone, and he began with "Gucci, we really appreciate you coming out. It was a real pleasure to meet you, and we really enjoyed getting to know you." As he was talking, I started to feel bad for him, because I could tell he was setting me up for a letdown.

I decided to jump in. I interrupted him and said, "Boss, I get it, no problem. I would love if I got to see you guys again next year." There was a pause on the line before, suddenly, in chorus the Boss and the other officers chanted together, "Welcome aboard, asshole!!" and then burst out laughing. I'd made the team. The culmination of years of hard work, sacrifice, and determination all came to fruition with one single prank. It was a classic move for a group of naval aviators, and through their laughter I smiled and began the next phase of my life, in a moment of pure Glad To Be Here.

REACHING THE DREAM AND JOINING THE TEAM

The interesting thing about being selected for the Blue Angels team is that—despite all my experience—I wasn't prepared for what was coming. My first flight with the Blues was absolutely transformational. It became a moment where my perspective completely shifted. My belief that I could fly with the team had taken me far, but I was on the cusp of another profound elevation that ultimately changed the way I thought about performance and achievement forever.

Once I was selected, life in those first few weeks in Pensacola, Florida, was simple: my job was to observe. I became what we call a "newbie." You don't speak in the debriefs, except to say,

"Glad to be here." You're low-key, and in the presence of this greatness you realize the power of humility. Being humble is what opens you up for improvement; and in order to be a part of this team, humility is exactly what you need. You've been selected; but it's not your time yet. You listen, you observe, and you ask questions; but it's not your place to comment or critique. Seeing if a newbie is dedicated enough to be humble is how the newbie's worth and trustworthiness are proven.

At some point, after weeks of observation, the elite culture started to take hold in me; I became part of it, and it became part of me. Finally, at one of the air shows, the Boss came up to me and asked, "Gucci, you wanna go flying today?" After weeks soaking up the surrounding factors that make the Blues an elite team, I was ready to take my first flight inside a blue-and-gold jet. Not a practice flight, but a real air show.

I suited up and took the back seat in Blue Angel #7, a special two-seat F-18 that the Blues use for training and to give VIP rides. For this flight, I was merely a passenger. We were actually flying the #7 as part of the demo, slotted into the four-jet diamond formation. My anticipation was physical and visceral. It was a bluebird day (clear blue skies), and when we strapped in I could look out over the thousands of spectators waving and cheering. The excitement made the hair stand up on the back of my neck.

Our canopies came down in unison. On engine start I felt the familiar rumble of the turbines spooling up. We went through the usual takeoff checks, and then things got challenging. We were lined up together, four jets on the runway packing 128,000 lbs of thrust, more horsepower than the entire starting lineup of the Indianapolis 500. (I've recently been on that track, standing on the bricks as the drivers got the call to start their engines.) That was the same kind of rumble you feel when you're in a formation of four F-18s all preparing for simultaneous takeoff—you can feel the asphalt rippling beneath your feet. I kept thinking, *This is it. I'm about to be inside an air show.* It wasn't just any takeoff or any air show; this was the Blue Angels. In that moment, I was overcome with the awe and excitement you feel when dreams come true.

On the runway we lined up, four jets across. I looked to either side, saw that our wingtips were nearly overlapping, and thought to myself, *Holy crap, we've got a problem here.* I'd been an instructor pilot, I'd done thousands of takeoffs, and I realized that if any one of us got a flat tire or the engine sucked up something from the runway, we'd end up with a lot of flames and metal, real quick. And then the thought hit my head, *Am I afraid?*

I can honestly tell you that in that moment, the answer was no—but I *was* scared, and I think there's a difference. Watch the next time you feel fear. Typically I say that fear is like a force coming at you; it feels like something outside of your control. Fear can cause you to get stuck, or even paralyzed. You can see this in yourself, in your teammates, and even in nations. But feeling scared is different. Scared is when those little hairs on the back of your neck stand at attention; it's a feeling that says, "Maybe I won't walk down this dark alley tonight." These are your instincts; trust them.

That day on the tarmac, I thought to myself, *Why am I not afraid? Why am I not freezing up right now?* The answer was that I had a deep trust and faith that we were going to make it. But, I wondered, where did *that* come from?

THE THREE P'S

I realized years later I was scared but not afraid because I had an intense belief in three things. I call them the three P's: people, process, and purpose.

First was my belief in the **people** around me. As I've mentioned, in addition to the six demonstration pilots, the Blue Angels include more than 110 individuals in support and maintenance roles. I knew that I could depend on everyone on the team—it's a very special feeling that all of us share.

I was not afraid because I had an intense belief in three things. I call them the three P's: people, process, and purpose.

Second was my belief in the **process**. The Blue Angels have been flying air shows since 1946. I'd been observing the team and I knew that their processes had been continually refined, and continue to be refined to this day.

Many organizations have those first two—or are striving for them—but that's not enough. The third P is a differentiator: **purpose**. There is a unique power in having a purpose and, I suggest, a purpose larger than self. That was the standard that held up each member of the Blue Angels, and allowed us to achieve at the highest levels. Everything we did reflected our sense of this elevated responsibility.

Once I established my belief, I was ready for takeoff. All four jets were lined up on the runway, and in each cockpit was a pilot, standing on the brakes, putting pressure on the top of the rudder pedals so they could run up the engines. I felt as though pure, raw power was about to take over. Each jet was poised like a coiled python, wound up and ready to strike. There was tension in all the airplanes, and finally the radio crackled with the Boss's voice: "Off brakes, now!" And on the "n" of "now," the tension was broken and the jets leapt forward in synchrony, gathering speed as one.

The Boss then bellowed, "Burners ready . . . now!" and the pilots jammed the throttles all the way forward to the firewall, engaging the full 128,000 lbs of thrust. It knocked me back in my seat as we leapt forward. In no time at all, 100 mph went by, then 160 mph, and we were propelled airborne.

When we were still only a few feet off the ground, the pilot swiftly dipped the left wing down, and we went slicing in underneath the wingtip of the #2 jet. The next thing I knew, I was underneath the afterburners of the Boss.

If you've ever been to an air show, you know how loud those jets are from the ground; now imagine being a mere 36 inches beneath another jet's afterburning engines. We were thundering through the sky when the Boss's voice again came on the radio: "Up . . . we . . . go!" On the "g" of "go," all four pilots smoothly pulled back on the stick and we went straight up into the vertical, rocketing away from the earth.

The afterburners were all around us and the flames of the lead jet's engines blew right in our faces; I was surrounded by metal; the airplane was shaking. In that moment, in between the awe and power, another thought hit me: *How am I going to do this? How am I going to fly this level of aerobatics so low to the ground and in formation?* You see, we flew in ways that day you wouldn't even attempt if you were by yourself at the safety of 10,000 feet. How was I going to perform with that kind of skill and intensity?

MESSAGE FROM THE ANGELS

That first flight sent me a message. In general, the closest a fighter pilot flies to another airplane is 10 feet (120 inches) in straight and level flight. And yet there we were, a diamond formation of four F-18s a mere 36 inches apart. From 10 feet to 36 inches—take all those factors together, in tight formation down close to the ground, and that's an "improvement" of 300%. What the Blue Angels were saying to me that day was, "John Foley, if you want to play in this game, you're going to have to raise your performance by 300%. We as a team and an organization are going to raise our performance by 300%, and guess what! You've got three months to do the same." *That's* the training cycle of the Blue Angels.

Now extend this analogy. Can you imagine what your business results would look like if you had that kind of improvement in three months? What would your numbers look like? What would your *life* look like if you had a 300% improvement in one quarter? That's the awareness of my potential that was unlocked in that first flight. I had achieved a great deal to get there, but in order to succeed, I was going to have to raise my belief levels yet again. I felt challenged and confident at the same time. It was time to button the chin strap; even in the world of elite fighter pilots, this was taking it to a whole new level.

I've told that story to professional athletes and coaches, to CEOs of Fortune 500 companies, and I can see the spark in their eyes when they start to understand that belief is the key to unlocking potential. Once you have that realization, the only question becomes: How good do you want to be? How do you make this real in your world? How do you activate the power and elevate a belief, both for yourself and for your team?

> *Your belief has to resonate with both the heart and the head*

GETTING FROM BELIEF TO REALITY

The first step is commitment. The path is going to take many twists—awareness, resilience, faith, perseverance, and of course hard work—but the key to opening this door is getting clear on your beliefs. First you have to paint the picture in your mind of what is possible. Your belief has to resonate with both the heart and the head. You should be able to feel it so that it becomes visceral, more than a mere thought. Then, you need to find extreme clarity and determine exactly what you want. It should be so clear that you can state your belief in one sentence.

After you clarify your existing beliefs, then you can focus on elevating those beliefs. This may lead you to ask: How do I actually raise belief levels?

Your belief levels can show you the trajectory of your aspirations and give you an awareness of what is possible. A clear awareness of potential, of what could be, is essential to elevating your beliefs. Growth comes from identifying and going beyond blind spots. We must overcome our ignorance. Ask yourself: How do I get from my current state to my future state? The space between those two ideas is something I call the High-Performance Zone. When you become aware of it, you put yourself in a position to elevate your current state and rapidly close the performance gap.

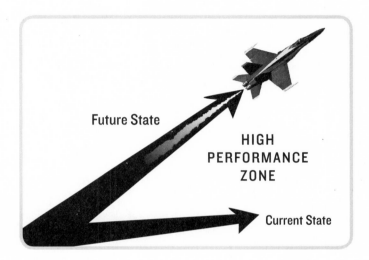

Understanding the correlation between belief and action is critical. If we limit ourselves to our current reality, we never achieve the level of the person who's able to see beyond the horizon, beyond the norm, beyond the top 1% of performers in their field. If you elevate your belief in what you are capable of doing, if you can realign your mind in order to see the extent of the possibility to improve, your performance will follow. It takes commitment and focus. There is no balance here. If you want to be the best, you have to be willing to push the limits. Don't just set your sights on general improvement; instead, push your belief to the absolute limit. It's at the limits of our current beliefs that excellence lies.

As far as examining your beliefs, I like to make a distinction between different types. I like to say that there are two kinds of beliefs: limiting and liberating. One holds us back, while the other leaps us forward. When you begin to break down the different types of belief in your life, you can begin to change them and make them work to your advantage.

Excellence lies at the limits of our current beliefs.

LIMITING BELIEFS

Limiting beliefs are ultimately grounded in fear. They cause us to look at the future—and at basic facts—with anxiety and doubt, largely focusing on factors outside our control. They can cause extreme stuckness and have a devastating effect on productivity, and even on personal happiness. Everyone is going to feel moments of doubt; but often, these kinds of doubt can be overcome with a shift in our perspective and beliefs. With strong conviction and effort, you can flip a limiting belief into a liberating belief. A potential threat can actually be an opportunity to improve and achieve results that extend far into the future.

That is exactly how I overcame the prevailing thought that I was too small to play Division 1 football. Yes, 5'9" is not the ideal size, but I never let that stop me. By focusing less on size—and more on speed, situation awareness, and sometimes just pure guts—I changed not only my perspective but also that of the coaches.

On the other hand, I could have taken it to an even higher level. When I look back at my football career, I can see the distinct effects of holding a limiting belief. My goal when I got to Annapolis was to make the traveling squad, which meant being first or second team. I made it to that squad, and I was even a multiple letterman, but I only periodically filled a starting role. I don't look back with regret, but knowing what I know now, I can see that I became complacent by achieving one goal and not resetting that goal to a higher one. Ultimately, that's what limited my success.

The key is to reset your goals before you actually achieve them. High performers are always improving and then resetting their goals. That's why I always felt at home in the Blue Angel culture. Our results are directly tied to our beliefs. They are either pulling us forward, or holding us back.

The key is to reset your goals before you actually achieve them.

LIBERATING BELIEFS

Liberating beliefs are empowering. They seek opportunity. This is where passion comes from. These beliefs cause you to look at the same less-than-ideal factors and instead of feeling fear, feeling a sense of responsibility and excitement about maximizing opportunities. This kind of belief has a continually positive effect on achieving goals. Liberating beliefs pull us forward. They liberate our performance and ground us in a positive mindset. Finding these beliefs can help you redirect your energy. The "Glad To Be Here" mindset fuels and accelerates these transformations.

I owe my current career to a liberating belief that guided me through a particularly challenging phase of my life. After spending some time working in venture capital, I caught the entrepreneurial bug and I decided to start my own business. When I was at Stanford, I had a vision for an entertainment company that would be like the NASCAR of aviation. I wanted to channel the thrill and power of an air show into a competitive environment. My experience in venture capital gave me confidence, and I decided to make that dream a reality.

Things started out powerfully, as I had the experience, knowledge, and connections to do what no one had been able to do before. I completely financed the initial seed funding myself, putting up a quarter-million dollars of my own money. In early September 2001, I flew to Manhattan to discuss an equity deal with ESPN and some other investors.

The day of our meeting turned out to be extremely significant, one that impacted our country very deeply: September 11, 2001. In the climate that followed, my deal totally collapsed. No one was going to invest in an aviation entertainment company after 9/11. This event had a deep and dramatic effect on many lives, our nation, and the world as a whole. It also had a big effect on my life. The dream of that opportunity evaporated, I was saddled with massive debt, and, shortly afterward, my sweetheart at the time broke up with me. To be honest, I

DIAMOND PERFORMANCE FRAMEWORK

1
BELIEF

- VISION
- INSPIRE
- COMMIT

CenterPoint®

was more hurt about that than losing the company. It was an extremely challenging time for me.

Despite my personal adversity, however, I didn't give up. In fact, I held a deep-seated belief that I could reinvent myself and achieve the success I was looking for. That belief was absolutely liberating. It kept me engaged with the world around me. It kept me from feeling self-pity, and instead focused me on seeking opportunity. At the time, I was deeply interested in growing personally, professionally, and spiritually. It was at an event—much like the ones I speak at today—that a light bulb went off.

That's when I started to translate my experience of seeking a 300% improvement—shooting for high performance—in leadership, teams, and business, and also in life mastery. That's the journey I'm still on today.

Liberating beliefs are part of the everyday mindset of extreme high performers. If you keep your eye on potential and opportunities, and focus on goodness, gratitude, and the small successes in your life, then you will begin to see the world differently. There is a theory called Hebb's rule that has been important in neuroscience for decades: neurons that fire together wire together. When you begin to associate liberating beliefs with positive action, you actually start to create new pathways in the brain. I believe that our thoughts are like electricity: they follow the path of least resistance. Defining our beliefs is a way to create new channels of less resistance, and thus to allow our thoughts and actions to liberate us.

As you begin to assess your beliefs, remember that this action does not exist in isolation. This is the first step in the Diamond Performance Framework, a cyclical process designed with continuous improvement in mind. With each cycle of the DPF, you reevaluate your beliefs, which puts you in a constant cycle of pushing the limits of what's achievable. And by doing this before you execute, you are elevating your actions. With elevated beliefs, you are ready to take the first steps toward elevated execution. This is a spiraling-up process that works in every aspect of life and all businesses.

3

Dynamic Focus:
Sharpening Your Mind

"Concentrate all your thoughts upon the work at hand.
The sun's rays do not burn until brought into focus."

—Alexander Graham Bell

Flying in formation at 36 inches requires even the most skilled pilots to elevate their beliefs. But that's only the beginning; 36 inches is the distance between Blue Angel jets in the formation at the beginning of the show season. During the year, through 270 days on the road and countless hours of heart-pounding, intensely physical flying, the team improves. We go from 36 inches on the first day down to just 18 inches by the end of the show season. Every day we improve, each flight better than the day before. Flying like that in close formation—100 feet off the ground, upside down, with the world streaking below at 500 mph—requires a special tool I call *dynamic focus*.

Dynamic focus is the ability to shift between the task at hand and the overall situation in fractions of a second. It creates rapid compartmentalization, followed by immediate execution. It is the ability to focus down and open up in cadence. This ability allows single-pointed focus along with total awareness. This is a skill that can be taught and mastered. It requires a special control of your mind and your actions. Think of it as the ability to perceive everything going on around you, followed by hyper-focus on a single task or variable. Hyper-focus is a necessary component of elite performance. But if you can both focus on and maintain a simultaneous awareness of the situation, you increase your ability to spot opportunities. This kind of mindset, geared toward elevated execution and improvement, is what sets apart elite athletes, innovators, and—at an extreme level—Blue Angel pilots. Our ability to focus in this way was another arrow in our quiver of high-performance tools. This is unique to the best of the best. It's what separates the professional from the All-Pro, and the All-Pro from the Hall of Fame.

Dynamic focus is the ability to shift between the task at hand and the overall situation in fractions of a second.

The ability to assess a situation quickly, make a decision, and take action is critical in any endeavor. Take, for example, a batter trying to hit a 100 mph fastball, or the IndyCar driver cornering at 232 mph. There's an assessment that takes place. The batter sees the pitch thrown; first assessment: Is it a strike? Then comes the swing or the check. It's the same for the driver; there's an assessment: What's my line, high or low? When do I brake, and when do I accelerate as I come out of the corner? The right split-second decision gives you the most speed on the optimum line.

> *Focus separates the professional from the All-Pro, and the All-Pro from the Hall of Fame.*

This is the same kind of split-second decision I made while executing the Knife-Edge Pass. As I'm flying straight toward another jet at 1000 mph closure, I'm making constant adjustments to stay on altitude, on flight line. At two miles, my wingman starts to appear in the distance in front of me, just a dot in my vision. As the milliseconds go by and we close on each other, I have to be aware of everything: Is there turbulence, are all my factors in the right place? When he's really close, at 100 feet, I'm aware of the nose position of his jet, even in a crosswind. Then, at the exact moment that we are about to pass, we both roll our jets 90 degrees, hard, with maximum stick deflection so that we barely pass each other, just a wingspan apart.

Dynamic focus also provides elite performers with a mindful awareness of the present moment. Instead of getting lost in specific details, it allows for quick scan patterns that identify what is important for achieving your immediate goals. It's like opening up the radar scope; for a brief moment, you assess everything that's coming at you, and then quickly focus your mind like a laser on what's important, both opportunities and threats. Dynamic focus does not stop when you finish a task; it is something you need to develop throughout each day and throughout your entire life. Great meditators know this extremely well. Great fighter pilots know this extremely well. Successful people in business and life also know this extremely well.

As a defensive back, I remember how this felt on the football field. Dynamic focus allows you to see the weight of the linemen shift as they lean on their heels for pass protection. It allows you to note the acceleration of each receiver and anticipate movement. It allows you to read a quarterback's eyes, all while maintaining situational awareness of the whole field and the hundreds of small cues that point to appropriate action. You need to make extremely small and fast corrections.

Maintaining both awareness and focus is even more challenging when you're landing jets on aircraft carriers. As you descend toward the pitching deck, there are countless variables, every one of them in constant flux. You have to develop a scan pattern with three primary focus points: the meatball, the lineup, and the angle of attack. The meatball is an optical landing system (an array of lights on the aircraft carrier) that guides pilots through the final phase of landing. You need to maintain a 3.5-degree glide slope and angle of attack, which has you coming down at about 750 feet per minute. At that speed, when you hit the deck, it feels like a controlled crash. But there's a saying in naval aviation: "Any landing you walk away from is a good landing."

Remember, the meatball is attached to the ship, and the ship is on the water. The deck is pitching up and down, constantly changing the position of the meatball, forcing thousands of slight corrections as you come in for landing.

After assessing the meatball, you assess the lineup. There's a centerline on the angle deck of the carrier. You need to land directly on this line because if you land just 15 feet off center, you will hit the other airplanes parked on the edge of the deck.

Third, you have to hold the angle of attack. That's the attitude of your nose as you come in to land. On a carrier you have to hold this attitude fixed so that the tail hook on your jet will catch one of the cables installed on the deck. If you were to slightly drop your nose or flare like on a normal civilian landing, the hook would skip over the cable, and you would not stop. The goal is to have all three variables in place. This is extremely hard, and almost never executed perfectly, but your goal is to achieve only minor deviation.

The closer you get to the deck, the quicker the scan pattern becomes. When you're farther out, say three-quarters to half a mile, you can make larger corrections. But when you get close, the corrections need to be extremely small and rapid. You fly the airplane all the way to touchdown, making numerous minute stick and throttle corrections. When you're about to land, you're moving so fast between each factor that you're simultaneously seeing all three at once. That's an example of dynamic focus.

DYNAMIC FOCUS IN THE BLUE ANGELS

If this tool is helpful in carrier landings, it is absolutely essential for the extremes of Blue Angel flying. Tucked up under the wing of another airplane, we have a few reference points that allow us to triangulate our position. The most important one is up above what we call the wing root, where the wing meets the fuselage. On every F-18, right there in the same spot, the name of the manufacturer is printed in gold letters. When you are in formation you can read these names. When I was flying, it read McDonnell Douglas, which was later acquired by Boeing. Depending on how the letters looked, we could tell how close we were in the formation and what adjustments needed to be made.

If I got deep (dropped too low), I would see the bottom of the letters disappear. If I went flat (too high), I'd see space below the bottom of the letters. If I was forward or aft, I'd see more letters appear or less of them disappear. By referencing the small changes in these letters, I was able to keep the jet within a three-inch circle. And don't forget, that is during loops, rolls, and even upside down. While this kind of task requires focus, it's not your only job. From inside the cockpit, the landscape changes in the blink of an eye. (At 500 mph you cover two football fields every second.) The formation moves slightly through changing winds and turbulence. You're straining your entire body, pulling multiple G's without a G-suit, and still you're able to give care and attention to the placement of a few small letters in your field of vision. That's the power of dynamic focus.

Having to rely on dynamic focus may sound a little overwhelming at first, but remember: it's a skill. It's something you have to develop over time, and the best way to do this is in real time—you have to start somewhere. These days we know that simulators, virtual reality, and visualization of actions can help, but when it comes to dynamic focus, you must start practicing in the real world. Experience matters. That's why athletes practice to the extremes they do; you have to train like you fight. Dynamic focus is a kind of extreme presence, being present under any circumstances.

I've had the privilege of sharing the stage a number of times with Michael Roach, the world's expert on the intersection of ancient wisdom and modern success. In his presentations, he makes a powerful analogy between the human mind and a video camera, as a way to illuminate why this skill is effective. The mind, it turns out, works a lot like a camera; that is, we think in frames at the rate of about 65 frames per second. The mind records everything, but slowing down the feed and understanding each of those frames is a task that requires a special kind of focus similar to the kind I've been describing in dynamic focus.

Dynamic focus is a kind of
extreme presence, being present
under any circumstances.

In every moment of our lives, these frames are flying from us at an incredible speed. But the trained mind—or even the untrained mind in extremis—can slow them down and focus on the critical elements of any situation. When you attain this kind of focus, it feels like reality slows down. But what's really happening, I believe, is that the mind is speeding up. You are activating more of its capacity. When you're flying in a Blue Angel air show, this makes the difference between simply *seeing* an airplane outside your canopy and *being aware* of the exact aspect, speed of closure, and even the cracks in the paint on the other jet. During this extreme focus you actually lose track of time. Your mind is so focused and present that you are in what I call the High-Performance Zone.

OTHER EXTREME ENVIRONMENTS

Of course, a finely honed ability to use dynamic focus is not limited to landing fighter jets on aircraft carriers. Over the years, I've spoken to other high performers who have lived this kind of focus in extreme situations. Team Penske, for example, is one of the most competitive teams in both the NASCAR and IndyCar circuits. In terms of speed and intensity, Team Penske has a lot in common with the Blue Angels. I've had the privilege of working with them in recent years.

One day I was in the garage talking with the mechanics, and in walked Helio Castroneves, one of Team Penske's star IndyCar drivers. He has the kind of bright, funny personality that spreads a natural feeling of Glad To Be Here everywhere he goes. He came in that day beaming with a huge smile. He walked straight up to me and started telling me about how the previous day he'd survived a heart-stopping crash. During practice laps preparing for the Indy 500, while moving at over 200 mph, the air got under the wing of his car.[8] The vehicle went completely airborne and inverted. Magically, he survived unscathed, and told me, "When I was upside down, flying through the air and feeling the G-force, I thought of you in the cockpit of your F-18." With that huge smile on his face, he hugged me. While

---

8 "Helio Castroneves Indianapolis Motor Speedway Incident May 13th," https://youtu.be/bQZOmnJKllU.

it's a funny story, I find it even more illuminating, because to have that kind of focus, to be aware of your thoughts even in the midst of a potentially fatal situation, *that* is what sets elite performers apart.

You may have noticed by now that many of the examples I use to illustrate my points tie directly to various types of extreme environments. I believe what we learn in extreme situations can apply in other areas, including our daily life. You may not be feeling the G-forces, and the consequences of your actions may never be as immediate as when you're traveling at 1000 mph, but if you zoom out, it's exactly the same trajectory. Every moment is precious, and every decision we make is of importance to our future. By understanding the kind of focused awareness that works in split-second, extreme situations, we can prepare to engage that awareness in our everyday lives.

In today's digital world, many of you might not have to stretch to make this comparison. There's so much information coming at us, such vast amounts of data available for analysis, that we need to be able to identify the important things first. Allowing ourselves to be overwhelmed by the constant flow of information that appears to be coming at us can become a distraction that compounds over time.

By understanding the kind of focused awareness that works in split-second, extreme situations, we can prepare to engage that awareness in our everyday lives.

Understanding this kind of focus is one thing. But how do you activate this skill and add it to your own repertoire? Beginning this process is as simple as starting to incorporate an awareness alongside your focused actions. But mastering this motion, and unlocking its full potential, requires that you bridge the two sides of this practice: unconscious competence and conscious ritual. Allow me to elaborate.

UNCONSCIOUS COMPETENCE

There's a link between dynamic focus, muscle memory, and the formation of automatic habits. Executing a task until it becomes a part of who we are is essential for maximizing the power of dynamic focus. Tasks for which we have acquired unconscious competence become habits that we execute without conscious effort.

> *When dynamic focus becomes second nature—habit—it influences our performance quickly and automatically.*

One way to understand unconscious competence is to examine unconscious actions, or habits, and the way they are formed in the brain. This can give us some insight into how dynamic focus helps individuals on teams like the Blue Angels execute at an extreme level. In his book *The Power of Habit*, Charles Duhigg demonstrates how recent discoveries in neuroscience have changed our understanding of the brain. Habits, it turns out, operate in a different part of the brain—one that doesn't require conscious effort. Neuroscientists have linked the process of habit formation to an area deep inside the brain called the *basal ganglia*, which also deals with elementary processes like voluntary motor functions and emotions.

Conscious decision-making, on the other hand, is handled in a completely different region of the brain called the *prefrontal cortex*. By habituating our actions, they actually bypass our conscious, decision-making mind and literally become second nature. This allows us to execute without taking time from the present conscious mind. That's the key to this practice. When dynamic focus becomes second nature—habit—it influences our performance quickly and automatically.

Forming unconscious habits takes will and determination, but the process that forms them is simple: repetition. A study published in the *European Journal of Social Psychology* found that on average, it took participants 66 days before an action became a habit. I was once discussing this concept with one of the top doctors at the Mayo Clinic. As we were talking, I asked him how many times it took for an action to become a habit. "John," he said, "you're asking the wrong question. What you really need to ask is 'What are you trying to do?'" His perspective is that the number will vary based on the complexity of the task. For something simple, let's say you want to drink a glass of water when you wake up every morning. Just remember to put a glass by your bed at night, and it will quickly become habit. To fly an F-18 through a Knife-Edge Pass—where two jets approach at 1000 mph closure and attempt to miss each other within a wingspan—it can take hundreds or even more than a thousand repetitions to hardwire the move into your response mechanisms.

The first few hundred times I did this—flinging my body and my aircraft at another individual in these extreme conditions—things were fast, and scary. But I quickly learned that the more I executed a task, no matter how extreme, the more things started to slow down. Having built the thought patterns that came with a mental focus and habitual practice, I was able to slow down the experience in my mind. Hardwiring habitual tasks allows you to execute effortlessly. You see beyond the motor functions and begin to see things at a much deeper level. The sensation is calm, yet exhilarating. Stable, yet dynamic. You start to sense a life force that seems to come from inside. You feel a thirst to repeat it, always knowing that you are operating on the edge.

Unconscious competence is what elite athletes mean when they refer to being "in the zone." They are not thinking about what they are doing. The precise mechanics, the right mindset, and the perfect actions are as natural to them as the beating of their own heart.

After I gave a talk on this, someone asked me, "What do you do if you're in formation and you have to sneeze?" The answer is: you don't sneeze. When you're in these incredibly focused states, you don't even get the urge to sneeze—until you relax. You're so focused and immersed in the present that you simply don't sneeze. The urge doesn't come. But if something did take your attention, we had a procedure to loosen up the formation so you could deal with the situation. The call over the radio was "Go well clear." That meant every pilot eased up the formation out to six feet so you could deal with the situation and clear the formation if needed. If you get something in your eye or if an engine catches fire, it's the same procedure. We built these default actions into our process, and they were the same for extreme and for normal activities. That's what made them repeatable.

While a commitment to practice is a prerequisite to being able to perform in the zone like this, it's only the first step. To achieve unconscious competence requires treating practice the way you treat live performances. That's how you make the great play, every time. I realized years later, when I began to speak about personal mastery, that it is through repetition, over time, that we are able to change the way we think, perceive, and execute. Small things done consistently over time drive major change. So go big in the small things.

This kind of building-block approach can help you master the unconscious side of dynamic focus, just like it did for me when I was a Blue Angel. It's exactly what I encountered during winter training on the Blues. I had already flown off carriers, been an instructor pilot, and engaged in dogfights. But when we got airborne for my first training flight as Blue Angel #6, my leader, Spurt (the lead solo pilot that year), told me we were going to start by learning to turn the smoke on and off. We did it once together. And we did it again. And again. He'd say, "You gotta match me." And we did it again. All of a sudden we were halfway through the flight, getting closer and closer to a synchronization, and I realized we were going to spend the whole flight working on smoke and timing patterns. I thought, *What the heck, is this all we're going to do?*

Go big in the small things.

I realized later Spurt was breaking me down, taking me back to the fundamentals in order to reach a different level of precision that wouldn't have been possible otherwise. We eventually got through 10, 20, finally 30 repetitions with the smoke before we moved on. From there, we practiced hundreds of timing patterns. These begin when you're three miles out on your checkpoint, and you take a mark. The next 20 seconds is the solo timing pattern. It's a descending turn to your three-mile checkpoint. You have to practice it so you get there on airspeed, on altitude—on time, every time. The following day, we added more complexity. Every day getting better, flying two airplanes, then four, then six. That's how you build an air show. One piece at a time.

And that's how you up your own game, or make strides toward the 300% improvement you're aiming for: one step, one action, at a time.

CONSCIOUS FOCUS: THE POWER OF RITUAL

The conscious side of focus begins with a ritual. Having a repeatable, dependable sequence of tasks puts you in a position to succeed. In the chapter on the brief, you'll learn the details of a foundational ritual that focused our minds and prepared us for extreme execution. But the brief was just one piece of the larger ritual that happened every day we flew.

When you go to an air show, you expect the pilots to be precise; our team is known for our visually stunning aerobatics. But one of the most striking things about the Blue Angels is how precise the ground crew is. Everything that happens in the organization—in the air, on the ground, or how the team acts in the world—is a reflection of the culture of excellence that has defined the Blues since our inception in 1946.

This culture starts with the support crew. They arrive at the show site early in the morning to prepare the jets. Along with fueling and basic maintenance, other duties require the crew to actually climb into the airplane, fire up the engines, and execute what are called "morning turns." They go through all the checks for each airplane: hydraulics, electrical, smoke, everything. Afterward, they can be seen taking rags and wiping the paint, polishing the wax, washing the windshield, and making sure every little bug is gone because at two miles out, a bug on the windshield can look like an approaching plane. The crew's ritual is so precise that when I enter the plane to fly the air show, I know everything will be in its exact position. My helmet is going to be perfectly placed on the side of the airplane. All the switches will be in the correct position. My flight gloves will be in the airplane sitting on the right-hand console, with the left glove draped over the right glove so that I can slip on the left one first.

The pilots never asked the crew to do all this prep, other than to simply have the jets ready to go. The crew took this seriously because they wanted to do a good job, and accordingly they created their own policies and procedures. They understood the objective, and they were empowered to get it done. They created their own method for upholding the incredibly high standards of the Blue Angels.

That's powerful. And that's the conscious side of dynamic focus, creating rituals that inspire elite execution.

CREATING YOUR TRIGGERS

A trigger is a tool that allows you to switch your mind into a higher zone. It's a personal tool that takes you beyond the ritual and elevates you to a higher state of awareness. It's a conscious bridge. The more I habituate my mind to clarity, the more I get into that zone. That's why triggers are such an important part of entering dynamic focus.

For the Blue Angels, our collective trigger was one of the steps on our preflight checklist: "Canopy down." We all lowered our canopies in synchronization, and as the canopy closed over the cockpit, all the other issues in one's mind took a back seat. This is extreme compartmentalization. Anyone on the team could have other issues on their mind—a report due, a personal challenge with their spouse or family, maybe even frustrations with someone on the team. But we trained our minds and bodies that the canopy coming down was a silencer for all those issues. When that canopy locked in, it was as though a vacuum sucked everything out of the cockpit so that our entire beings—mentally, emotionally, physically—could shift into a high-performance mindset. For the next 45 minutes, we knew life was defined by the thundering noise and the punishing G-force of a Blue Angel air show. We were ready for anything.

Compartmentalization is essential to focus, and your trigger is the bridge that locks you into that mode. This is true for anyone performing at the highest level. I once asked my friend Russ Francis, a three-time Pro Bowl tight end, if he had any triggers. "I know exactly what you mean," he said. "Mine was the chin strap." He then explained that as his team ran out of the tunnel and onto the field, he'd always button the chin strap of his helmet right at the moment he crossed the goal line. The snap of the second button locking into place was the moment when his mind blocked out all other thoughts and distractions, and his entire being focused its resources on the game at hand.

That's what a self-imposed trigger is for: to instantly marshal your whole body and mind into the optimal "fight" mode with hyper-focus only on what matters most. In those moments, you don't try to hype yourself into taking the right action. You just react—mind, body, and spirit as one—because your mind has been trained to enter a state of pure execution and focus.

The difference between simply hyping ourselves up and activating a trigger is *conscious process*. A trigger is not a good luck charm, or something you pull out when necessary; instead, it's something you've predefined and worked into your daily actions. I encourage you to create an actual ritual for use in your daily life that includes triggers, like the canopy coming down, or the chin strap getting buckled. If you work in a field where precision matters—for example, a surgeon or an athlete—you will already be familiar with this process. A surgeon approached me after a talk once and said, "There's a difference between you and me. If you make a mistake, you die; if I make a mistake, the patient dies."

There are so many different examples of triggers. For a teacher, it could be the moment when the first student enters the classroom. For a writer, it could be the moment that you block out the internet and focus in on your work session. Finding something that's unique to your experience, however, has real staying power. Personally, I always get out of bed with my left foot hitting the floor first. This reminds me not to get complacent about how special this world is and how precious each day becomes. I try not to see things as normal, but to see the magic and awe that surrounds us.

A key to performing at the highest level is to train yourself to automatically react in the most optimum way, no matter what the circumstances or stakes. Creating a trigger will help you activate your performance. But there's another approach that can actually change the way you see the world around you. That's the territory of the 0.01%—the absolute best of the best.

> *I try not to see things as normal, but to see the magic and awe that surrounds us.*

THE GLAD TO BE HERE WAKE-UP: PROACTIVE FOCUS

Preparing a proactive ritual can elevate your performance in work or life. I'd like to share with you one of the most important rituals that I use every day. I call it the "Glad To Be Here Wake-Up."

Since my time flying, the Glad To Be Here mindset has become something so much larger than I ever could have imagined. It's the secret sauce that has the power to transform the way we see the world and deepen our impact and relationships with everyone around us. When we are actively grateful, it creates new pathways in our minds and changes the way we see and understand the world. A grateful mindset changes our perspective. It helps us spot opportunities to help others and to realize our own success. It can boost our potential to be creative or to innovate. Gratitude changes the game and changes your world. Tapping into this mindset on a daily basis is critical for anyone pursuing higher performance. It can even improve your physical health. A number of studies at UC Davis have indicated that daily interactions with gratitude led to a 28% decrease in perceived stress, and a 23% decrease in stress hormones such as cortisol.[9]

Gratitude changes the game and changes your world.

Here is a simple exercise you can do every day to get your mind habituated to this idea. The goal of this practice is simple: align your first thoughts each day on the things for which you are grateful. This creates a positive effect that lasts throughout the day and throughout your life. Here's how I engage this mindset in three simple steps.

STEP 1: PRESENT

The first thing I do every morning is think about what I am grateful for. I do this while still in bed. I bask in the idea of being alive and in good health, and on all goodness that surrounds me in the moment. I go over the specifics of my current surroundings, and the amazing people in my life that make all of this possible. I say thank you multiple times.

---

9   "Gratitude is good medicine," *UC Davis*, November 25, 2015, http://www.ucdmc. ucdavis.edu/welcome/features/2015-2016/11/20151125_gratitude.html.

STEP 2: PAST

I reflect on the past 24 hours and recall events and people I am thankful for. I do this by frames, starting with my wake-up from the day before. Again, I am reliving and basking in any goodness done or observed. It's fun and can sometimes continue for a while, depending on the day. You can go back as far as you want, to your parents, a teacher, or someone who made a big impact on your life. But since I do this every day, I use 24 hours as a starting point. It doesn't have to be an act of goodness you've done. When we observe someone else bringing joy into the world, we receive part of that benefit.

STEP 3: FUTURE

Now comes the part that can impact others: planting seeds for the next 24 hours. I think ahead to the upcoming day in frames of the events and people. Here is where exchanging self with others comes into play. I try to think of what they will need or want, and then plant the mental seeds that they receive it . . . or maybe I can actually do something to help them get what they desire. The key here is thinking of others and visualizing actions to benefit them.

You can repeat each of these steps throughout the day. It's also powerful to use this ritual in the evening and fall asleep in that grateful state of mind. This aligns your mind on a grateful state while you rest. I have a favorite quote that has stood the test of time: "If your prayer is thank you, that's enough" (Meister Eckhart). This ritual is a small endeavor, but it just might be enough to effect a real change in your life.

If you do this regularly, it will transform the way you feel.

It can even change the way that other people perceive you. Recently someone told me that I have a childlike exuberance that is a joy to be around. I started thinking about it and I've noticed that same thing in others around me. That state of mind, to me, is exactly the result of making this ritual a habit. Your gratitude and your thankfulness change not only the way you perceive the world, but also the way the world perceives you.

Unconscious competence, conscious ritual, and proactive focus are all ways to engage in elevated execution. These approaches do more than maintain the necessary attitude and perception of high performance. It's a form of gestalt, where the whole is greater than the sum of its parts.

Your gratitude and your thankfulness change not only the way you perceive the world, but also the way the world perceives you.

Elite techniques like dynamic focus will have an immediate impact on your performance. Even if you want to achieve elite performance, however, it's just one small piece of a larger process. Developing extreme focus is only one of the ways the Blue Angels prepare for an air show.

4

The Brief:
Connect, Align, Commit

"By failing to prepare, we are preparing to fail."
—Benjamin Franklin

On the day of an air show, anticipation hangs in the air. Long lines of cars gradually snake around the show site and begin to fill the massive parking areas. People gather on the tarmac by the tens of thousands. There is joy and excitement in their hearts. On the airfield, all kinds of modern fighters and an array of historic aircraft are exhibited in the static display area. Children with awe shining in their eyes push to see them up close. Meanwhile, somewhere on the base, beyond the joy and the anticipation, there is a small room with a makeshift sign on the door that says "Blue Angels Only." How intimidating is that? If you're on duty walking the halls of the base and you see that sign, trust me, you're not going into that room, no matter what your rank.

Behind that door—in small rooms around the country and the world—the team and I gathered before every flight to brief our upcoming performance. It's a ritual we practiced every single day. Sometimes we flew multiple times per day during the 16-week preseason and additional 32-week show season. Every one of those flights was preceded by a brief. I recently looked back at my logbook and saw I flew 120 training flights before our first air show. We averaged 10 flights a week during the show season, over 440 flights per year. That's what it took to hone our brand of razor's-edge proficiency. It didn't matter how successful our previous show had been; we'd be in the briefing room again the very next day going through the sequence of events, preparing our minds as if it were the first show of the year.

We called this practice "the brief," and at first blush, that's a good descriptor. But from the first time I set foot in the sacred space of the Blue Angel briefing room, I could tell—immediately, instinctively—that these elite performers were engaged in something different. For the Blues, briefing was more than a meeting and more than a habit; it was a capstone event with the seriousness of a sacred ritual.

When something takes on the significance of ritual, it connects you to your belief and makes a more powerful impression on the brain. While a repetitive event like a Monday meeting can be useful, it's different from the kind of brief the Angels hold. What makes the Angels' brief a ritual is *how* we did it. It wasn't something you simply showed up for; we had to mentally prepare ourselves for what was coming, to ignite the higher conscious elements of our minds. This would give us the edge we needed to perform magic in a changing, inherently unforgiving environment. The brief is so important to maintaining peak performance during an air show that if you missed it, you didn't fly that day.

The briefing was a capstone event with the seriousness of a sacred ritual.

The brief is the place where you take your focused, elevated beliefs and turn them into consistent, efficient actions. The brief stimulates communication, creates alignment, and most of all, focuses the entire team. One of the perennial challenges for the Blue Angels is to create an awesome, extreme, thrilling experience that is not only effective, but also safe for the massive crowds in attendance. Achieving these two aims is both difficult and essential. The brief was a key habit where we made certain both would happen. It allowed us to see safety and operational excellence as two sides of the same coin.

Each time I entered the Blue Angel briefing room, we were moments away from executing a mission that would take every ounce of physical and mental strength I had. It was imperative that we separate ourselves from the distraction of the gathering crowd. The briefing room was our office on the road. We put up the sign on the door because inside that room we needed to create a safe environment to bear down, focus, and relax—yes, *relax*—before pushing our aircraft and ourselves to the absolute limit. Outside the briefing room, our standards were impeccable; but inside, we loosened up a bit. We were a family on the road, and we needed a place to work, recharge, and reconnect on a personal and professional level.

By the time the pilots entered the briefing room, the maintenance crew had it set up with a large table in the center and the digital screens we used to review flight footage. We all arrived around the same time, put down our briefcases, unzipped our flight suits, and mentally prepared for the ritual ahead. The pilots sat around the table in order, #1 through 8, gathered like the Knights of the Round Table. On the edges of the room were chairs for the support officers and any guests we might have. There was both a serious tension and a joyful togetherness.

The environment we created in the brief served multiple purposes. First, it was a structured forum for communication and alignment. But there was a second, more powerful element here that few really understood. There was a cadence, a discipline to this ritual. Many businesses have a mechanism like this—like weekly or quarterly reviews—but what we did was additive. We created the environment where focused preparation enabled elite execution. That unlocked a quickening of the mind, a doorway where you could access deep focus. We were always trying to get the most out of every action we took, and the brief was critical to our success.

We created the environment where focused preparation enabled elite execution.

The moment we stepped outside the briefing room, our performance began. You could see the level of focus in the way we carried ourselves. Our flight suits were zipped and we were completely prepared for the precise, synchronized march to the crowd line. Every member of the team exuded our core mission: to be the best of the best; to be the boldest, most exciting flight demonstration squadron in the world; and most importantly, to represent our nation, our citizens, and our fellow service members as ambassadors of goodwill. It may come as a surprise that this was our highest mission; yet it played out every day both on the ground and in the air.

We executed this ritual with seriousness because our lives depended on this kind of process. But you don't have to be flying in formation to benefit from this practice; this kind of preparation can elevate the actions of any individual or team. I remember the way my defensive-back coach at Navy would always tell us, "If you're not getting better, you're getting worse!" This has proved true throughout my life. If your goal is continuous improvement, feedback matters. The brief and debrief combination is a crucial part of the DPF. Combining the two creates a feedback loop that lets you take everything you've learned and apply it to the actions you're about to take.

Now, let's step into a Blue Angel brief and look at some of the elements that made this ritual unique.

THE BRIEF: A SACRED RITUAL

The brief is a gathering where your team connects, aligns, and commits to results. Think of it as a tool for preparation and focus. At face value it might seem familiar—all organizations use some type of brief that is systematic, iterative, and focused on outcomes. But the Blue Angel process I'm going to describe is different because of the emphasis on mental preparation.

DIAMOND PERFORMANCE FRAMEWORK

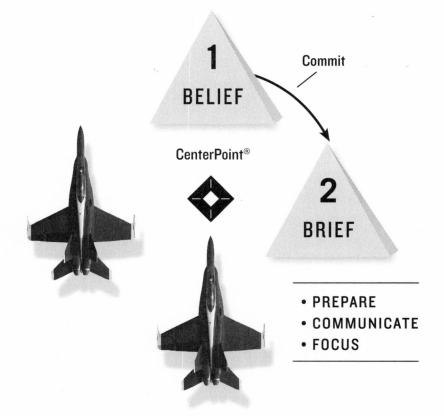

This is a ritual gathering that employs specific tactics, including visualizing outcomes and the actions needed to reach them. These tactics create the speed teams need to perform at their absolute highest potential. The brief is an arena where you bridge the gaps between operational excellence, flexibility, and speed in decision-making. Great athletes, surgeons, and stage performers all know this. Most successful people relate to this.

The brief is an arena where you bridge the gaps between operational excellence, flexibility, and speed in decision-making.

Traditionally, briefing meetings are meant to be quick and efficient. Yet there are plenty of scenarios that are important enough to require slowing the review down. If you're facing a must-win situation, like a finalist pitch or a bake-off to decide which investment bank will take your IPO, you need to be prepared to an extreme degree. Or, if you're simply seeking to get a greater return on every action, the brief I describe is a differentiator that will set your team apart.

We all perform actions like this informally or subconsciously when we think about an upcoming task. Our minds put us in the environment and we make some quick assumptions that formulate our expectations. Giving structure to this allows individuals or teams to address more variables, consider the actions, and experience the desired outcomes. This allows everyone to pay more attention to the details, establish clearer expectations, and gain confidence. This alone improves performance and creates a higher level of belief.

When I think of the brief, I always remember something my dad used to say to me as a child. Whenever I started to stray, act up, or be late for something, he would tell me, "Get with the program." Even as a kid, I knew that meant I'd gotten out of the parameters and I needed to check myself. There are standards of performance (SOPs) in any group, and there are also tolerances to those standards that form a kind of buffer, like having guardrails on the left and the right sides. You still have to stay on the road, but the boundaries are defined. The brief is a space where we are constantly reminded of those boundaries, where they are both articulated and recognized. Briefing together creates collective understanding and keeps expectations aligned.

It's important to remember that the brief is not a planning exercise; it is a tool for preparation and focus. SOPs are something that are defined outside of the brief. When you come into the brief, you already have a plan. On the Blues, we already knew which maneuvers we were going to execute, and exactly how they were going to happen. The goal of the meeting, then, was to bring collective preparation and focus to future actions.

Briefing together creates collective understanding and keeps expectations aligned.

The same is true whether you're working with a team, or if you're applying this process to your individual performance.

Although you come in with a plan, the brief also provides a foundation for adaptability. Whether you're flying an air show or leading a company, adapting to change is essential. Yet the ability to lead through change is even more important. In any situation, things change. On the Blues, we had to adapt the air show to the local terrain hundreds of times a year. We flew four days at every show site, and each show was unique. They contained the same core maneuvers, but given the local terrain, we usually had to adapt. We flew in changing landscapes: through cities, over water, around bridges; we had to account for physical obstacles like skyscrapers, mountains, and power lines. Even when we nailed down the particulars of a show site, the weather and the winds could change—and frequently did—sometimes in the middle of a show. We briefed the plan, but we always understood that the minute we got airborne, things change.

Whether you're flying an air show or leading a company, adapting to change is essential. Yet the ability to lead through change is even more important.

These kinds of "extra-mile" habits are what distinguish elite performers. The brief allowed us to carry out our performances safely and effectively. Through the lens of continuous improvement, we focused on outcomes, which inspired the growth mindset that defined our culture. Our goal was to get better every day, and to execute with greater precision. Getting buy-in to a new way of interacting can be a challenge for leaders and team members.

I often think back to my first Blue Angel brief. As soon as I was in the room, I knew it was going to be different. Yes, it covered the same criteria I had used in my fighter squadrons, but something was different. The intensity, the focus, and the chemistry were at a whole new level. Making the transition took work, but these elevated expectations shaped who I became for the team and who I am today. I believed in the people, the process, and our purpose.

This is one of the things that bind elite performers together:

a deep connection to each other, to the mission, and to a higher purpose. They have a thirst for knowledge, and they thrive on sharing information—on learning from each other. At the most basic level, what these elite performers are doing is connecting, aligning, and committing.

PART ONE: CONNECT

There are three main goals in an effective brief. At its core, the first goal is simple: connect. Teams thrive on connection, and the brief is a natural place to strengthen those bonds and keep everyone moving in the same direction. Additionally, any project or action contains multitudes of moving parts and pieces; the brief is a space where you connect the dots between those ideas for your upcoming performance. It doesn't have to happen in person—my current team employs a system of virtual briefs and debriefs—but the key is that people need to connect at a human level. It also doesn't have to happen every day, though that's how it works for the Blue Angels. On the other hand, a brief can happen multiple times in one day if your situation calls for it. For example, if you're handling multiple in-person sales pitches, you might brief before each meeting. That's the key mechanism to keep in mind here: the brief happens immediately before you take action, and it's used to bring increased focus and efficiency to that action.

At a basic level, elite performers connect, align, and commit.

An effective brief is built on a solid foundation. Above all, it is a safe environment, where everyone has input, ownership, and respect. Later, in the chapter on debrief, we'll describe the precise dynamics that define every high-performance brief or debrief. For now, it's enough to know that the brief is an arena for genuine human connection with clarity of objectives and priorities.

The opening sequence of a Blue Angel brief would be familiar to anyone who has spent time in the military or in business. We go through basic procedural items, with separate sections led by the Boss, the operations officer, and the safety officer. Every show site was different, so it was essential we set the tone for the event and brought group alignment and awareness to the exact show we were about to fly. Regardless of where we were flying, safety took priority. Safety was reinforced in every briefing, including a group recitation of an IAE (Immediate Action Emergency) protocol. We would recite in synchronization, from memory, the immediate action steps for, say, an engine fire during flight:

1. Throttles—Minimum practical Single FIRE light or Dual when side confirmed

2. Throttle affected engine—OFF

3. FIRE light affected engine—PUSH

4. FIRE EXTGH READY light—PUSH AND HOLD UNTIL DISCH LIGHT COMES ON[10]

Going over these as a group heightened their importance. Even though we had more flight hours than most pilots, we

---

10 NATOPS Flight Manual, Navy Model F/A-18E/F 165533 and Up Aircraft, p. 496.

went back to the basics we'd learned in flight training. At the elite level, fundamentals matter. Another way we highlighted safety was by isolating different aspects. One was general awareness, but then we got more detailed when there were site-specific obstacles that needed to be addressed. Sometimes a tower was close to the flight line, or something was happening with the weather, or we had a long distance to cover to reach our emergency landing field.

At the elite level, fundamentals matter.

After basic procedures were covered, we got very specific. We worked from aerial photos and reviewed the exact flight path and geometry of each show. We drew flight lines with one-, two-, and three-mile checkpoints. Then we made reference points in front of and behind the crowd line and at 30-degree angles off the flight line. This geometry standardized how we were going to fly and how we were going to communicate, with specific reference to the geography. This is one example of how we took complex situations and broke them down into solvable components. Then we layered those components on top of each other until we had an awesome product. This is consistent with how Einstein and today's top physicists attempt to solve complex challenges. First, you break things down to the smallest component, solve for that, and then build back up.

The one-, two-, and three-mile checkpoints we identified make the timing of each maneuver possible. In preparation for a maneuver like the Knife-Edge Pass, it's essential to establish accurate checkpoints. "Accurate" might be an understatement. I still remember the first time I was exposed to the extreme precision of these checkpoints. I was the new #6, the opposing solo.

When we arrived at a show site on Thursday, we had to take the aerial photograph, the map of our air show, and imprint that into our brains. The way we did that was by breaking up into twos and following each other along the flight lines so that we could determine our checkpoints. This engrained them into our visual memory. We called it flying "circle and arrival."

During one training flight, we were flying a circle and arrival and I was trailing in my jet a couple hundred feet behind the current lead solo pilot, Spurt. We flew over the CenterPoint about 200 feet off the ground and we started our stopwatches, timing nine seconds—at 400 knots ground speed (a knot is about 1.15 mph) we were doing a mile every nine seconds. Yes, it's a cool feeling to go that fast so close to the ground. At the end of nine seconds we looked 90 degrees off our shoulder, to the left or right, to find the one-mile checkpoint—something we could see from the cockpit. It might be a road intersection, a building, a tree—anything that would give us a precise point of reference.

As we were flying that day, Spurt was radioing the information back to me. He said, "Gucci, one-mile checkpoint: the road intersection below." Another nine seconds, and he said, "Gucci, two-mile checkpoint: let's use the white house." Actually what he said was, "Gucci, two-mile checkpoint, northeast corner, three-story white house, the upper window with the green shade."

Did you catch the specificity of that second checkpoint? The first time I heard Spurt point out a checkpoint that precise I couldn't even see the house, let alone the green shade in the upper window. I was absolutely blown away, but I would learn later how important it was to be specific. Put yourself in the cockpit for a second. Imagine the world flying by you at 400 knots, 200 feet off the ground. There's another F-18 hurtling toward you at the same speed. That's a mile of closure every 4.5 seconds. How do you achieve the clarity of mind that you can see the green shade of a window while flying upside down that fast, and that close to the ground? Getting to this level of clarity requires both a focused mind and the preparation that the brief process delivers.

These are some of the specifics that we cover in a Blue Angel brief. When you apply this process yourself, you are going to brief on different specifics. I shared some of our key elements to give you a look inside the air show, and to demonstrate how specific we got when we did our preshow planning. As for what you discuss, the upcoming action will define the specifics. This is not where you decide what the specifics are; rather, this is where you connect and get focused for the performance ahead.

PART TWO: ALIGN

Once the basic plan has been outlined by the specifics, it's time to align actions. By taking a small amount of time to create unified action and focus, you're increasing the speed of your overall performance.

In order to align for the heart-racing performance that lay ahead in our Blue Angel shows, we did something that few would imagine: we executed a group visualization. This element illuminates an approach to performance that makes elite teams unique. These are the subtleties that make the best even better. Navy SEALS employ a similar process; if you break it down, you can find this practice used in elite teams of all varieties. It's sometimes called a "walk-through." On the football field, teams walk through different coverages and formations. A pit crew in training will walk through tire changes and simulate the whole pit stop. Even children's sports teams learn from these kinds of techniques.

What these group walk-throughs have in common is they take an individual's focus and synchronize it within the team context. But elite teams take this practice to a whole new level. On the Blue Angels, we took these visualizations as seriously as the flight.

During the visualization, we all sat around the table in the briefing room. Then the Boss led us through the entire air show, starting with the march down to the jets. He voiced his calls with the same voice, and even the exact tone that he would use later in the air. He modulated the inflections in his voice to emphasize the intensity of certain moments in the air show, like when the team is flying toward the bottom of a loop, the earth is coming up into your windscreen, and the Boss needs to keep the planes behind him from hitting a low bottom. So when he makes the call "A little more pullll," there is a fluctuation in his voice that makes you realize it's coming harder. The intensity in his call influences our actions.

It is also crucial that the Boss maintains an overall consistency in his delivery. The goal of the visualization is to recreate the exact experience of what we're expecting to hear and feel in the cockpit. That way when you're in the air and things do change, which they always did, you can pick up on the subtlety in his calls and understand what's different.

The goal of the visualization is to recreate the exact experience of what we're expecting to hear and feel.

While the Boss led us through the sequence, some of us would close our eyes. Others would mimic moving the stick like they'd move it in the airplane. If you could look inside each of our heads, you would see us picturing what was going to happen in minute detail. During these moments I found myself entering a state of pure focus that I discovered later in life is consistent with high-level meditation. I had to be able to see multiple things in a fast, effective, precise way. I could see the "McDonnell Douglas" letters spelled out on the airplane. I could reference the key indicators in my heads-up display. I could actually see the cracks in the paint on the jet beside me. I looked over my shoulder at the exact moment, and I could see the green shade in the upper window of the white house we'd identified earlier. There was a tone and texture to the Boss's voice that put my mind right in the cockpit. I became so immersed in these sessions that I could feel the G-force and sense the rush of the earth flying up into my windscreen. These visualizations were emotional, contextual, and visceral. They brought us into an emotional state that is exactly the same as it would be in the cockpit. The more you can do that, the better the results of the visualization will be. That detail gave them an even greater impact on the performance to come.

Anecdotally we knew the value of these visualizations for our performance, but as I later learned, the power of visualization is rooted in the nature of the brain. Research into visualization practice shows that what we were doing was more than just preparation. Through repetition, we were actually changing the way our minds focused, carving new pathways in our brains that allowed us to execute at higher levels. The detailed way we visualized it actually created mental impressions and planted seeds for our future success.

I've had the opportunity over the years to talk about high performance with a range of firsthand experts. I was skiing recently with Billy Kidd—the legendary World Cup skier who became the first American man to win an Olympic silver medal in alpine skiing. As we were riding up the chairlift and swapping stories from the Olympics and air shows, I mentioned how we would visualize before every flight. He told me they would do the same thing, and that in his experience, visualization had the same benefits I had noted. Before a race, he and the other skiers would visualize the entire course in real time, just like the Blues. They would time themselves, and those who were best at it finished the visualization within tenths of a second of a two-minute run time.

Scientific research conducted over the last century backs this up. As far back as 1932, studies have indicated that visualizing the outcome of your actions can have a significant impact on execution.[11] In more recent years, scans of the brain have showed that simply visualizing an action has an effect on the brain that is very similar to actually performing the action.

The sports world knows this practice well. Trials have consistently shown that athletes who add a mental training regimen outperform those who use only physical training. It is now commonplace in every elite program. Furthermore, scans

---

11 "Electrophysiology of Mental Activities," Edmund Jacobson, *The American Journal of Psychology*, vol. 44, no. 4, October 1932, https://www.jstor.org/stable/1414531.

of the brain have revealed that when you visualize an action, it activates and develops areas of the brain that address problem-solving related to the action being visualized. One study even demonstrates that individuals can increase a skill to some degree through mental practice alone.[12] That's what makes this a powerful ritual. Visualization is a technique to help actualize the future. It is—like the brief overall—a tool for preparation and focus.

> *Visualization is a technique to help actualize the future.*

This skill will benefit anyone, not just F-18 pilots or competitive athletes. We all naturally do this without any training, albeit to a lesser extent. If we're about to have a difficult conversation, we mull over what we plan to say, and picture it at the same time. If we need to drive to an unfamiliar location, we picture the route in our mind—at least I do. When you realize your mind is active in this task already, the question becomes: How do I benefit from this? How can I focus on this natural tendency of my mind, and amp it up to the next level in order to get prepared in the best possible way?

Visualization is something I still engage with on a daily basis. Each year I do more than 100 speaking engagements. I could probably deliver certain speeches at the drop of a hat if

---

12 "Modulation of muscle responses evoked by transcranial magnetic stimulation during the acquisition of new fine motor skills," https://www.ncbi.nlm.nih.gov/pubmed/7500130 and http://drdavidhamilton.com/does-your-brain-distinguish-real-from-imaginary/.

I needed to. Nevertheless, I consistently wake up early on the morning of giving a keynote address. This way, I give myself an extra couple of hours to go through my entire presentation in my head. I meticulously picture each step of the sequence I've planned: what I'm going to say, how I'm going to say it, and most importantly, how I'm going to make it meaningful for my audience.

There's a big difference between going over your steps in a last-minute rush, and calmly visualizing each step toward completion. At this stage in my career, I'm not worried that I'm going to forget a point in my storyboard, or get the order of my slides mixed up. What I'm practicing is the ability to adjust, quickly and seamlessly, playing off the crowd's reaction and creating an impactful experience. Visualization helps me habituate preparation so that I can flow onstage and be fully engaged with the audience. The focus is on them, not me.

Visualization can't guarantee me a perfect outcome on the stage. What it can do, however, is align my thoughts with the upcoming performance. That's the power of this phase of the brief. Aligning thoughts and actions well before the performance activates an attention you can call on quickly when needed, as soon as the performance begins.

PART THREE: COMMIT

Every great leader on this planet can tell you they wouldn't be able to move forward without commitment and buy-in from their team. Engaged individuals drive efficient and collective action. At a high level, the brief is a formalized place to establish commitment. It is crucial that a brief conclude with defined commitments. This is an important step that cements alignment, creating a clarity that allows the team to move into execution.

> *Aligning thoughts and actions well before the performance activates an attention you can call on quickly when needed, as soon as the performance begins.*

A Blue Angel brief is a place where we are making all sorts of high-level commitments to one another. We promise to execute each maneuver in the precise sequence and timing. We make a game plan for contingencies. And overall, we create the feeling that everyone is ready to go and 100% engaged.

Each individual in the brief has a photo of the show site. We've already prepared each photo with our flight lines and checkpoints mapped out; but in the brief, we're rehashing these points and making commitments to follow them precisely. When I say I'm going to be on my checkpoint, exactly on time and on speed, these are commitments that build high trust. As the season progresses, each brief and each promise bring new opportunities to reinforce trust. Clarity on the small things matters in the brief, just as it does in life. Small things matter when creating trust, and we have to earn the trust of our teammates every day.

For leaders, recognizing commitment in your team is a matter of emotional intelligence. That makes this pursuit a little more elusive, but there are steps you can take to ensure that every brief ends this way. Overall, it's crucial that the brief be a safe and open environment. A single opinion that goes unvoiced can have a negative effect on individual commitment, and ultimately affect the performance of the team as a whole. If anyone leaves the brief feeling unsure of their role or responsibilities, you're going to degrade the benefits of focus and synchronization with the team. That's why it's crucial that the brief be a 100% safe environment.

As a leader, you have the power to set the tone of each meeting. It is your responsibility to empower, incorporate, and discuss dissenting opinions. On the other hand, as a non-leading participant, it is your responsibility to speak up, and to make sure that you can leave each briefing with a confident commitment to your actions. That means putting everything on the table and allowing yourself to engage with the team environment completely, without holding back.

Commitments and personal contracts are such an important part of elite teams that their effects and presence extend well beyond the brief. The formation of definite contracts between individuals is a main component of the DPF, and the subject of an upcoming chapter.

You might be thinking: *Well, this all sounds good, but you can't force personal commitment.* But remember, the brief is one piece of a larger process. The Diamond Performance Framework is designed to create a natural feedback loop, which inspires commitment and action. Every brief is eventually followed by a debrief. In the debrief, we are not only asking what happened, we're examining the personal commitments we made in the brief. What went well? What could have gone better? Was there anything out of parameters, and where could I improve? That knowledge comes into the next brief, which again goes through the process of debrief.

The direct line that connects brief to debrief goes through the CenterPoint, which is a unifier for the entire DPF. Now that you are aligned, prepared, and focused, you're ready for action. It's time to execute at the highest level through a CenterPoint and high-trust contracts.

5

CenterPoint:
The Power of Purpose

"A small body of determined spirits fired by an unquenchable faith in their mission can alter history."

—Gandhi

Blue Angel demo pilots are maximum-performance operators. The air show pushes the human body and mind to the absolute limit. The maneuvers we do are more daring and more demanding than any other flight demonstration squadron in the world. It takes intense physical strength and sharp mental acuity. Up in the sky, in our cockpits, we are focused and intense. But down below, what the audience experiences is a graceful flow of aerobatics and human connection.

Thousands of moving parts allow this to happen, almost none of which are in plain view. The communication and coordination that makes the air show possible is mostly obscured to the observer. It happens on the back radio, and in our briefing meetings. There are safety concerns, flight waivers, logistical planning, and thousands of other items that have to be checked off before the show begins. After we've flown a particular air show, it starts all over again when we move to a new show site. While you won't ever see much of this as a spectator, if you pay close attention, you can perceive that there's one tool we use that is always in plain sight. It's called the "CenterPoint."

Every maneuver in the air show is based on the CenterPoint. It's a physical point in space, somewhere on the airfield, marked by a white tractor-trailer on land or a certain boat on the water. To members in the audience, the white tractor-trailer parked on the grass might not look important, but to us demo pilots, the CenterPoint informs the decisions that we make.

Above all else, a CenterPoint is used as a reference point. It's a decision-making tool.

When you give it the importance we did during an air show, it lends all your actions a sense of deeper focus. It provides you with a sense of "true north" that allows you to react quickly in changing situations. It keeps individuals and teams focused on specific goals and outcomes.

A CenterPoint is a decision-making tool.

When you zoom in and examine the air show at a technical level, you'll notice that the flight team operates as two units: the diamond formation and the opposing solos. To achieve a fast-paced air show, we alternate maneuvers one after the other. As one unit clears the flight line, the other enters immediately.

The CenterPoint is right on that flight line, directly in front of the audience. Our goal during the show is to have constant action in front of the crowd. Closing the gap between maneuvers is something we worked on during the entire show season, and the show actually goes from 45 minutes down to 37 by the end of the season, as we get better and strive to give the audience a constant flow of excitement. Additionally, separating into two units allows us to showcase the many different skills of Navy pilots and demonstrate the F-18's varied capabilities.

The diamond unit consists of planes 1 to 4. They are led by the Boss and operate as a single formation, flying most of the show with all four planes moving as one, 36 to 18 inches apart. The diamond is the definition of synchronized formation flying.

The other unit, the opposing solos, are the maximum-performance demonstrators. While the diamond exemplifies the grace and precision of the F-18, the solos are tasked with pushing the human being and its airplane to the absolute limits. I can tell you from experience, this is intense flying. We ride so heavy on the afterburner and use up so much fuel that the air show basically has to end when it does because the solos have run out of gas. We used to joke that we were scorching around with our hair on fire—but that's back when I had a lot more hair!

Through most of the show, each unit operates independently, like teams within the team. But at the end of the show, all six of us come together to execute the final maneuvers as one single delta formation. This includes one of the most impressive maneuvers of the air show: the Loop-Break-Cross. This maneuver is the perfect example of CenterPoint alignment.

Before this maneuver even begins, the solos face one of the

most challenging parts of the air show: the rendezvous with the diamond formation. The Loop-Break-Cross is preceded by a maneuver that separates the solos from the diamond; as a solo pilot, I have a matter of seconds to cover a few miles, catch up with, and then join the diamond formation that is traveling over 460 mph. To get there, I'm gunning the afterburner, going as fast as I can without breaking the sound barrier (that close to the ground, you don't want to shatter all the windows in the parking area).

I aim for a closure rate of 150 knots, or 172 mph; a lot faster than the 10–20 knots closure in a typical fleet rendezvous. It might not sound that fast, but imagine pulling into a parking place at over 150 mph and then stopping on a dime; that's what it feels like to rendezvous with the diamond. As I approach, I'm flying proactively ahead of the formation along a calculated angle of approach. At the precise moment, just when it feels like I'm going to collide with the formation, I have to "porpoise the airplane." This is what we call one of the most punishing things you can do to your body inside a jet. As other planes fly up in my windscreen, I slam the stick back into my lap and take 6 or 7 positive G's of force, which crushes my body into the ejection seat. As soon as those G's take hold, I push the stick completely forward to create negative G—meaning I go from full positive to full negative.

The first time I did this, it really opened my eyes, literally! At 2.7 negative G's, it feels like your eyeballs are being pushed out of their sockets. I have to compensate for the negative G-force by relaxing my body, but this is exactly the opposite of what I need to do for positive G, which is to bear down and squeeze my whole body, starting with my legs, then gut, then chest.

When you porpoise the plane, you're taking both positive and negative G, back and forth. It's a dance between man and machine, an exchange of strength that I have to execute rapidly if I'm to stay on the flight path and bleed off energy simultaneously. Time is of the essence. If you're not in position when the Boss makes the call to begin the next maneuver, you have to clear the formation. But that rarely happens on the Blues. When the last solo pilot calls on the radio, "You've got #6, Boss," then the Boss makes the call, "Up we go," everyone pulls up in unison, and the maneuver begins.

In order to make the planes look seamless and maintain the 36 inches in the delta formation, I have to start pulling on the stick before I see the planes around me move. This takes extreme trust that can only come from a proactive mindset, which is essential for execution on the Blues. As I ease the nose of the jet up into the loop, we're going 440 knots, and taking 4 G's—which compresses the body. Speed gradually decreases when we break the horizon as one.

Smoothly, we're all flying upside down, still in tight formation, each pilot making constant micro adjustments to stay that way. It's a spectacular moment, hanging upside down together, with the earth under your head. But there's no time to admire the view; soon we're pointed straight down, rushing toward the runway and the crowd. At an exact microsecond, the Boss makes the call, "Smoke on, ready break!" and all six jets break away in different directions. We bolt out along our designated flight lines, looking out for our checkpoints.

Even though we're putting six miles of separation between the planes, we're still flying in reference to the Boss here, listening for his calls. Each one tells you precisely where he is, and how fast he's moving. A few seconds pass. My grip on the stick tightens. He calls, "Two mile, 420 knots, mark" at the same moment I'm passing my two-mile checkpoint. A few more seconds pass. Finally, as we all approach our three-mile checkpoint, the Boss calls, "Up we go," and I force the stick back in my lap again. To turn back in the direction I just came, I execute a Half-Cuban-Eight, where I go straight up over the top of the horizon, point my nose toward the ground, and then slam the stick to the left to roll my wings level.

Now all six jets are in separate corners heading straight for each other on precise flight lines that intersect at the CenterPoint. In the approach, I follow a specific scan pattern: What's my airspeed? Where is my checkpoint? Where are the other planes? What's my altitude? I'm still listening for the Boss. His call comes in, "Two-mile mark," though maybe I haven't quite reached my checkpoint. *Damn*, I think, *time to add a little power*. At this point, we're still four miles apart, but a skilled pilot can begin to see the shape of the other planes coming in at 1000 mph closure. I pass my one-mile checkpoint just before the Boss makes the call, "One-mile mark."

And perhaps I'm slightly off again. *Damn*, I think, *I added too much before*. So I take a little power off.

As I pass this checkpoint, it's only 4.5 seconds before the jets intercept. What happens next, when it's done correctly, is one of the most dazzling moments of the entire air show. The crowd can see it coming, all the jets hurtling toward one another. It looks like we're on a collision course, but what the crowd doesn't know is we are at slightly different altitudes. Suddenly, in a stunning image, we cross paths in front of the crowd in a six-plane stack. If you draw a line through the center of that stack, it will come down exactly on the tractor-trailer we've placed on the airfield that represents the CenterPoint.

It's a demonstration of Blue Angel precision, timing, communication, and commitment—and it's built entirely around the CenterPoint.

CENTERPOINT: BEYOND THE PHYSICAL

To the Blues, the CenterPoint is a dot in space. It's purely physical. It helps us align maneuvers and execute with precision. While that is important, that's not all this tool has to offer. Years later when I began to break down the keys to our success, I began to see the CenterPoint as something much bigger.

Depending on your goals and your environment, CenterPoints can take different forms. I often like to break them down into two categories: tactical and strategic.

Tactical CenterPoints relate to immediate actions. This could be something like a release date for an IT solution, or a sales goal. Key actions and priorities need to revolve around that CenterPoint. On the top you stack all the related elements and teams: sales, marketing, operations, HR, and admin. When everyone is aligned, the result is group execution by collective action. That's exactly what sets elite teams apart.

CenterPoints break down into two basic forms: tactical and strategic.

Strategic CenterPoints, on the other hand, are larger and have a wider scope. These are represented by the occasions on which businesses define their core values or create mission statements. While they still need to be defined specifically, our actions are tied broadly to strategic CenterPoints. They inform not only **how** you're executing but also **why**. They provide guidance for making decisions in any situation, big or small.

An example I use in many businesses is the customer. The customer is a CenterPoint that can clarify action in all kinds of situations. The nature of your business comes into play here. For example, in healthcare, focusing on the patient becomes especially important, because you're talking about patient-centered care and safety. When the focus of every action you take is directed at the patient outcomes—at sustaining life with compassion—your actions take on a special kind of power.

Strategic CenterPoints are often focused on core values. When you stack your core values one on top of the other, your actions move through them, giving you clarity and purpose. That's exactly how we operated on the Blues. The way we flew was related to our culture and our character. It was our desire to inspire greatness in others. The Blue Angel air show is legendary because everyone on the team is 100% all in, all the time. It's more than a professional commitment; it's a commitment of every ounce of your heart and soul. We get better as time goes on because everyone has a thirst for improvement, a deep desire for perfection; we know we may never get there, but we continue to strive.

Those core values centered our actions, but more than anything it was our purpose larger than self—to serve as ambassadors of goodwill—that aligned us. This was at the very core of our strategic CenterPoint. We knew we were representing more than the Navy or the Marine Corps; what I felt we represented was the potential of the human spirit, the greatness and goodness of humankind.

This higher purpose aligned our minds and brought focus to our actions inside and outside the cockpit. It defined who we were as individuals. We had many tactical CenterPoints, but for me, everything came back to our role as ambassadors of goodwill. This took many different forms throughout my three years and was defined by more than upholding the excellent tradition of precision air shows.

This higher purpose aligned our minds and brought focus to our actions inside and outside the cockpit.

For me personally, this role gave me a burning desire to inspire hopes and dreams in others. But for all of us, this CenterPoint is what drove us to find ways to serve the communities in every city we visited. While we were traveling across the United States throughout the show season, we routinely visited children's hospitals and worked with local chapters of the Make-A-Wish Foundation. It drove us to spend quality time with the families of children facing extreme obstacles. That was part of our mission, part of why we put so much effort into the air show, part of why we woke up every day and lived a Glad To Be Here mindset. We wanted to strengthen the bonds in communities throughout the country.

While we acted as ambassadors of goodwill every day, there was one episode where this role stood out most clearly. It began in 1992, the day we flew our Navy F-18s into Kubinka air base in Moscow to perform an air show with the Russians. This was historic in its timing and impact. The Berlin Wall had just come down in 1989. Countries were changing at their foundations. We had an opportunity to do something historic and we seized it. It was a rare chance to collaborate with the Russian military and the Russian people. In fact, we were the first US military squadron to pass through the iron curtain that had separated us all for decades.

Being ambassadors of goodwill defined everything we did from the moment we entered Russian airspace. We always knew the higher tenets we represented were not bound by borders or culture, and this trip was an amazing opportunity to extend our role beyond the borders of the United States and NATO. As we entered Russian airspace, we were reaching out to a people who had been our competitor only a few years before. We took the first steps toward reaching for common ground, *together*.

Our arrival was remarkable. We flew into Russian airspace in formation, approaching the border from Finland. As we flew over the Baltic Sea, I remember the anticipation. When we left Finnish airspace, we were handed off to Russian air control. I remember the check-in distinctly. The Boss called over the radio, "Moscow Center, this is Blue Angel 1, flight of 8, flight level 300." The answer came back, "Blue Angel 1, Moscow Center, what type of aircraft are you?" The Boss called back, "Eight US Navy F-18s." We waited for a reply. Then we waited a little longer. There was an unbearably long pause before they finally came back. "Roger that—continue."

I'll never forget flying over Russian territory that day. As usual, my mind was glued to flying in formation with the team, but my thoughts were reeling with where we were and what it meant. I was seeing imagery from two world wars, the Cold War, and the fall of the Berlin Wall. These scenes were from a land and a people that had been our ally, then our biggest opponent, and now it felt as though we were coming back full circle.

The Boss came on the radio. "Gucci, bogeys 2 o'clock, 40 miles, closing."

"Contact," I said, "looks like our escort coming to meet us." As operations officer, I coordinated with the Russians to intercept us and then escort us into Kubinka air base. But I wasn't prepared for the magnitude of the moment. Right there on my radar scope was not one or two, but four of the most advanced Russian fighters heading toward us at supersonic speed. I'd experienced this scenario in combat training, and now it was actually happening. I needed to remind myself that this was a peaceful engagement. But still, the little hairs were standing straight up on the back of my neck.

I called on the radio as the Russian fighters approached, "Tallyho! Ten miles, flight of four."[13] The Russian formation split and started a rendezvous on our wing. That was a sight I'll never forget, two Su-27s and two MiG-29s attempting to join on the outpost. We held our position smoothly, and they joined as expertly as any US fighter would have. I looked over my left shoulder and saw the visor of the Russian pilot in a

---

13 Because of an international agreement, air traffic controllers communicate in English.

brand-new Su-27. It was so cool. I waved to him and he waved back. Thumper, my fellow Blue, came up on the back radio. "Gucci," he said, "pay attention, we're still in formation." I said, "Roger that." But it was hard not to look, as it was so magnificent, such a rare sight.

As we descended toward the runway at Kubinka, I noticed a few things right away. First off, there was one large runway, very wide, about twice the width of our normal runways. The centerline, which had been freshly painted for our arrival, was a little bit squiggly. The runway was built of large, interconnecting cement blocks that allowed the cement to freeze and thaw without cracking. Some of them had large gaps between them. As I touched down, I was shocked at the beating our landing gear was taking from these gaps. It almost felt like the hard bang of a carrier landing, but this was at an airfield. *Well,* I thought, *that's why the Russian jets have such big tires and strong landing gear!*

Once we were on the ground, there was no mistaking the importance of this occasion. We taxied our jets into an incredible scene of pomp and circumstance—flags snapping in the wind and dignitaries in full dress uniform, standing at attention. As we left our jets and took our first steps on Russian soil, nothing felt ordinary. Right away, there was an air of importance. A Russian military band was playing a warbling, heartfelt rendition of the US national anthem. I was impressed that they had learned it! The Russian pilots were lined up in formation across from us. Everything was very formal. The band started marching. We stood in formation and saluted as they passed.

Then, within seconds, the Russian pilots came over and

started shaking our hands down the line, like two sports teams at the end of a match. As we shook hands with the pilots, the formality eased and things became joyous. The pace of the music quickened. Troupes of Russian dancers in full traditional garb grabbed us and we all started dancing on the tarmac of Kubinka air base. Then we did a formal Russian breaking-of-the-bread ceremony. Next thing I knew, we were surrounded by schoolchildren, smiling and bright. They assembled and said in a loud chorus, "Welcome to Russia, Blue Angels!"

The festivities gradually faded and we were escorted into the base, to our briefing room. We prepared for the first major part of our visit: the flight exchanges. As per our arrangement with the Russians, the leader of the Russian team was going to fly first with the Boss in a two-seat F-18. Then, I would fly the top Russian fighter pilot in our other two-seat jet. After that, we'd get a chance to take a couple of flights in the Russian jets.

There was a seriousness and gravity when we briefed with the Russian contingent. But when we finally walked down to the jets where we got to engage with our fellow pilots, everything changed. We were like kids on a playground—no language barriers or cultural differences could impede our shared love of flying. The mood was exuberant and infused with an attitude of "Glad To Be Here."

There in front of me on the tarmac were the custom-painted Su-27s and MiG-29s of the Red Knights, the Russian demonstration team. I couldn't believe we were this close to the Russian fighter planes; even more, I couldn't believe we were about to fly in them.

After the first couple of formal rides, things opened up. It was almost a total free-for-all; as fast as the jets could get gassed up, we were flying the Russians and they were flying us. Every aviator who had wings got to ride in and fly a Russian airplane. It was a free-spirited atmosphere of pilots being pilots, shaking hands, hugging, and sharing stories as best we could through the language barrier.

After I'd given the first official ride and was back on the tarmac, one pilot grabbed me and said, "Come fly with me." As we walked toward his airplane, I slowly realized it was an Su-25, not the top-of-the-line Su-27 Flanker or an MiG-29 Fulcrum. I almost didn't want to take the ride, but he was so excited to share his joy of flying with me that I jumped in anyway. It was my first experience inside a Russian fighter, and it turned out to be an amazing flight.

A TEST OF OUR MISSION

We were still riding high the next day when we kicked off preparations for the air show. The mood changed, however, when we received some bad news. A Russian general approached me and said, "Small problem"—a phrase that needs no interpretation to understand. Whether you're in the United States or in Russia, "small problem" translates into a big wrench about to be thrown into your plans.

"Small problem," he said again. "The airspace behind the Moscow beltway is a no-fly zone. Your squadron can't use it for your show."

The air show was to take place over an arena on the outskirts of Moscow. As operations officer, I had spent the previous weeks and months setting up our flight plan, which required a five-nautical-mile radius around the designated

CenterPoint. Moscow has a highway system much like the Beltway in Washington, DC, and our CenterPoint was right on the edge of it. Most of our flight maneuvers depended on having that area inside the beltway to rendezvous the jets in between maneuvers.

I'd been told well before we left the United States that we had clearance for the airspace we needed. Now, only two days before we were scheduled to fly, the general was taking away 50% of the airspace.

I responded with my first reaction to this news. "Sir," I said, "that's not acceptable. We absolutely need this airspace—you're going to have to get clearance for us."

He listened to me and went over to this phone—a heavy, old-fashioned rotary model—picked it up, and started yelling into it. I thought, *Wow, this guy is great—he's on our side, and he's going to get this thing done for us.*

But to my surprise, after he finished booming into the phone, he turned to me and said, "Sorry—I couldn't get it done."

(The next day, as it turned out, I had to use that same phone and realized quickly that he hadn't been shouting as a measure of his authority; rather, the connection was all but inaudible, and he was yelling into the phone just to be heard.)

At the time, of course, I was not happy about his response. Here I thought this guy was taking care of it, and in reality he couldn't get it done. Our position was "We need the full airspace. Period." It moved up the chain of command, beyond the military, to the top political officials in Moscow. Each time, we were met with a negative. Ever since a Cessna had landed in Red Square back in 1987, to the chagrin of the Russian military, the airspace surrounding Moscow had been declared a no-fly zone, much the same as the United States did around the White House after 9/11.[14]

We had two options, neither of which was good. Thinking they would bend first, we put our collective foot down and said, "Fine—we're not flying." The Russian response to this was, "Fine. Don't fly." This meant they would do the air show themselves and the Blue Angels—international representatives of US goodwill and foreign policy—would look like jerks for coming all that way and not flying. So either we wouldn't fly, or we had to modify our show. This may sound like a small thing, but making such a change would go against a long-standing protocol that said we did not modify our air show mid-season. I can't recall that this was ever done, even when we were flying in the United States.

The decision was weighing on us that night. We knew we had to find a way to fly the show. This situation put one of the core principles of the team—to fly the safest possible air show—in direct opposition with our CenterPoint, to act as ambassadors of goodwill. In our debrief that day, we discussed our options, trying to find a solution that would satisfy everyone. We basically came to a stalemate because it was not really a discussion for the whole team. So, without a game plan, the Boss and I continued to discuss it over dinner, analyzing the risks, weighing the consequences. I remember the Boss looking at me and saying, "Gucci, what do you think? What maneuvers can the solos do, even with the restrictions?"

---

14 In 1987, West German teenager Mathias Rust drew international attention when he flew a Cessna from Helsinki to Moscow and landed in Red Square. https://en.wikipedia.org/wiki/Mathias_Rust.

> *This situation put one of the core principles of the team—to fly the safest possible air show—in direct opposition with our CenterPoint, to act as ambassadors of goodwill.*

I thought for a while before something clicked, and I said, "Boss, we can do it. What if we started the air show head on? We'll do the opposing 360."

His eyes lit up; and then he said, "We'll bring the diamond from the right with the Diamond Pass."

"Right," I said, "and then we'll come in with the Knife-Edge." He countered with the Delta Roll; I came right back with "solos will enter the flight line crowd-right in the 'Fortus' formation," where Thumper and I fly as one with our gear extended—myself flying upside down to match Thumper's right side up. Before we knew it, we had sketched out a modified sequence on the back of a bar napkin. It had some of the same maneuvers, but with a new sequence to adapt to the changed requirements resulting from the airspace constraints.

It was going to take leadership and guts, but we knew this was what we had to do to uphold our strategic CenterPoint. This kind of last-minute restriction of our airspace would have been cause for the cancellation of a regular stateside air show. Without that innate desire to act above all else as ambassadors of goodwill, we might have simply canceled at Kubinka. But in that instance, the higher CenterPoint we'd committed to overruled some of our tactical protocols. We decided not to cancel because we found an alternate way to achieve our goal that didn't compromise safety. As long as we could keep it safe, we could proceed. Safety was one thing we could never compromise.

That's what lies behind the elevated actions of elite teams. CenterPoint alignment binds your actions and ensures that even in changing, extreme conditions, there's a benchmark that allows you to execute at the highest level. The Center-Point unifies focus and allows the team to spot opportunities for advancement and improvement that would otherwise go unnoticed. This kind of central drive is common to high-performance teams and individuals of all types, in sports, in business, and in life. It comes back to your core being. It makes you think on a daily basis about what drives your actions and why you do what you do.

The CenterPoint unifies focus and allows the team to spot opportunities for advancement and improvement that would otherwise go unnoticed.

MISSION ACCOMPLISHED

It was an incredible experience, getting a bird's-eye view of Moscow at the beginning of the post-Soviet era. Flying our air show over the buildings and streets of that city was surreal for me, and over the years I've heard from people who were in the crowd and had the same experience. Only a few months ago, I met a woman who told me she'd been at that Russian show as a little girl. She stood in Red Square and watched her country share its jets, its airspace, and its audience with us.

I asked her what it was like.

She told me, "It was amazing—and a very big deal for Russia. We were about two years into all the changes after the Berlin Wall came down. It was a beautiful time—people were open to new possibilities, hopes, and dreams. You guys represented that to me, and to all of us."

Her story took me back to the first time I watched the Blue Angels. I'd seen the same thing in them as she had—possibilities for a bright future. I saw warriors aligned and driven toward a common cause whose depth and singular focus I would only come to understand after I'd flown with the team myself.

A strong strategic CenterPoint can have an effect on every action you take, driving results and outcomes you could never have imagined without it.

Aside from my fond memories of this rare experience, it was our experience of mission that really stuck with me. A strategic CenterPoint is exactly the kind of central unity that you need if your goal is to perform at the highest levels. Remember, a CenterPoint is more than a dot in space. A strong strategic CenterPoint can have an effect on every action you take, driving results and outcomes you could never have imagined without it.

LOCATING THE CENTERPOINT IN YOUR BUSINESS

While the idea is large, and the implications are huge, this is something you can easily engage with. As a start with a new business client, I often encourage leaders to ask their teams, "What's our CenterPoint?" and see what kind of replies they get. Tight-knit elite teams know immediately and instinctively what point their actions revolve around.

There can be multiple CenterPoints in an organization, and they can shift, but the key is clarity and understanding. You could say the CenterPoint is sales, the customer, or our core values. None of those are right or wrong at that moment, but once you get to the context it becomes very specific. If your context is around core values, or if you're in healthcare, for example, it might be patient experience, then the whole thing becomes very specific.

The power of identifying your CenterPoint is also vital for an individual. Ask yourself, "What is the CenterPoint of my life? What is the one thing that all of my actions flow through, that informs key decisions I make?" Understanding with clarity where your priorities lie is a powerful awareness to take with you on this journey. This is the mindset of elite performers.

6

High Trust:
The Key to Execution

*"Trust is the glue of life . . . it's the foundational
principle that holds all relationships."*
—Stephen R. Covey

In pursuit of elite execution, you have a full quiver of arrows
from which to pull. But I often ask leaders, "If you had only
one arrow, which would you pick? What would your primary
focus be? Which tool would you choose to achieve that goal of
increased execution?" In my experience as a member of multiple elite teams, and in working with hundreds of organizations
around the world, I choose trust. I believe that if you increase
trust, execution will follow.

The Blue Angels are one of the greatest living examples
of how trust enables elite execution. Up in the sky, in tight

formation, we're holding the life of every teammate in the stick between our legs. The air show is built on countless moments where small mistakes have big consequences. In order to survive, we need to execute with precision and we have to trust—on our lives—that our teammates will do the same.

I believe that if you increase trust, execution will follow.

In the realm of business and high-performance teams, as well as in life and relationships, trust is one of the most important variables, if not the one irreplaceable component, for reaching greater success. Trust is fundamental and remains one of the crucial differentiators in all aspects of life. This is because trust is an essential element in every single group effort on this planet.

You don't have to be a member of an elite team to see how trust affects you. Even in everyday life the stakes are high. Trust underlies many of the basic things we take for granted in society. We wouldn't even be able to go to a doctor if we didn't trust that they were qualified and skilled. We wouldn't be able to drive on a two-lane road without trusting that both parties will stay in their lanes. This unspoken agreement between two drivers is the same kind of nonverbal contract that Thumper and I used to execute a Knife-Edge Pass. We both trusted that the other would stay on time and on flight line. And I can tell you one thing: when you're hurtling toward another jet at 1000 mph closure, set to cross within a wingspan, you need to trust the person in the other jet!

Trust gives us a clarity of mind that allows us to focus our energy.

High trust is one of the foundational elements of the Blue Angel culture. It gives us a clarity of mind that allows us to focus our energy on performing at the highest level possible. It allows us to fly closer together and lower to the ground than any other team in the world—safely. It allows us to accelerate and push boundaries that we wouldn't normally be able to push. High trust is the medium in which all of our daily interactions take place. It is something we work on constantly; we have to actively earn that trust every day. And it took form in what I like to call "high-trust contracts."

High-trust contracts are the foundation for communication in high-performing teams. It can be easier to trust in a safe and functional environment, but when things are not right, communication is crucial. You need to be aware of what the problems are, especially when things are off.

When everything is going right while flying a Knife-Edge Pass, the pilots' radios are mostly silent. But when things are off, communication becomes extremely important. As we're getting into position for the maneuver, my wingman and I have to perfectly nail the solo timing pattern. Then, to start the maneuver,

I come on the radio and ask my wingman one simple question: "Are you ready to take a mark?" At this point, we're six miles apart, well outside of visual range. What I'm asking with that question is "Are you in position, and are you ready to go?" The contract we had was that he could say no if he wasn't ready. Ninety-nine out of 100 times, Thumper was ready. But when he wasn't, I really needed to know.

High trust contracts are the foundation for communication in high-performing teams.

Once he responds "ready to take a mark," I call on the radio, "Standby, mark it!" and we hit our stopwatches. From that moment we both have 20 seconds to reach our three-mile checkpoint, on altitude, on airspeed, and on time. If he is at the three-mile checkpoint on time, he tells me nothing because the contract we have is: if you're on, you don't say anything. (On a side note, this contract can also decrease your voicemail and email.) If he's even one second off, he's late, and I need to know that, because it's the leader who has to correct. My contract to him was "I'll be right on the flight line, I'll set the altitude, and I'll make the timing correction." As my wingman, he has only one job: miss me. It was like the biggest game of chicken you ever played, but it was different because we had discipline and contracts. This is just one example of the high-trust contracts we used for precise execution.

THE THREE C'S OF TRUST

Before we examine the points where trust is formed, it's important to understand what makes someone trustworthy. When I'm trying to paint a picture of high trust, I often think back to the Blue Angel maintenance crew. When I joined the team, it was the first time I didn't do my own preflight checks of the airplane. Each day, I came out of the brief and marched to my jet with the other pilots. My crew chief would be waiting beside the aircraft. He would salute me, shake my hand, and say, "Sir, the jet is ready to go."

He didn't give me a long litany of the things they had done, or the challenges they had encountered. Because of the trust between us, this simple statement stood in for all of that. After we shook hands, I'd climb in the cockpit, look down, and see my flight gloves on the right console in exactly the same position every day, left over right. I would scan the cockpit to quickly ensure that all the switches on the F-18 were in exactly the correct positions. The radio was set, not only to the correct frequency, but also to the volume that I preferred. When the crew chief was preparing the jet, I knew he had gotten down on his hands and knees and counted the rivets on the ejection seat to make sure the rudder pedals and the seat were in the exact position I liked.

These details were important, but it was more than that. The maintenance crew had been out there long before us, starting the engines—those "morning turns." This involves warming up every system on the airplane: the hydraulics, the electrical, the flight controls. Every control surface was tested before I even approached the airplane. Any discrepancies were identified and corrected well before I had even arrived at the airfield. I didn't ask for any of that. The maintenance team and crew chiefs always went above and beyond. Does your team do that? What would it look like if they did?

In any other squadron, I'd be out there long before takeoff doing the preflight myself—but on the Blues we changed this. We empowered and trusted our crew chiefs to do it for us. That required extra training, but in the end created greater efficiencies for the entire organization. To trust someone on this level meant that your life depended on them doing their job. But the differentiator was that everybody went above and beyond. It wasn't just my crew chiefs—Joe and Pete—it was every crew chief on every airplane. The maintenance department created the processes, but the "whatever it takes" culture and the commitment of every team member was something that existed throughout the entire organization. All of this was achieved with high-trust contracts. This gave me the opportunity to be even more effective during the flight because it was one less task I had to worry about.

As I reflect back on those relationships, I ask myself why I trusted those around me so deeply. How were we all able to trust at this level? What were our crew chiefs doing that was different? When I break it down, I believe there are three main components that underlie these trust contracts. I call them the three C's of high trust.

I. **Competence**—The root of this concept is basic: Are you trained and do you have the necessary skills? Are you capable of doing the job that you've been assigned? Do you have the character necessary to do the right thing, even when no one is watching? Your character is defined by all the actions you take, and competencies are continually built throughout a career. You attend schools and receive training, but at the end of the day you need experience. Experience matters. The good news is that competency can be determined very quickly. We do this all the time, not only when you're hiring but also when you're assigning people to certain roles. To trust in their success, you need to know that they possess the skills, training, and experience to execute on those roles—and eventually to master them. Competency is the easiest element of high trust, both to identify and to achieve.

2. **Commitment**—When identifying this element, we're talking about more than basic commitment to your role. For high trust, you have to know that everyone is all in, that they are executing with 100% engagement. Commitment means being that person that everyone can count on—the one who's called upon when the most challenging situations arise, and the one who is looking out for others. On the Blues, this was a prerequisite for every member. All the Blue Angels are the embodiment of deep commitment. We all traveled on the road and spent 270 days a year away from home. For everyone, the team came first in our lives—before birthdays, holidays, or anniversaries. Families have to buy into it too, and at times that can really be hard. Flying with the team wasn't a nine-to-five job; it was a full-time commitment to a higher purpose, to a purpose larger than self. When mission comes over self, high trust becomes possible.

3. **Consistency**—This is the differentiator that separates the elite from others and allows for sustained high performance. It allows you to build on your performance every day. Consistency creates predictability. Do you bring your A-game to work every day? Are you consistent in both actions and reactions? How someone reacts under pressure is critical. Some people are calm under pressure, and others aren't. It's important to know how someone reacts not just when things are going well, but when you hit turbulence, not only in business, but in life. This becomes apparent as you work alongside someone. You have to quickly determine that they're dependable and consistent. Having both is what allowed us to fly in tight formation, because we knew how people would respond. When we're in the air, we have to trust that—no matter what, even when your engine is on fire—you're going to stay consistent with the procedures and protocols.

CONTRACTS: WHERE TRUST MEETS ACTION

Teams need trust in order to execute at the highest levels. But how do you build this high trust? Where does it come from?

Trust functions like an invisible network that touches every person in an organization. But trust isn't a complete intangible; when you focus on developing trust, you focus on the tangible pieces, on the visible manifestations of trust. There are places where the flow of information and collaboration have the potential to increase and thereby elevate an entire organization. At these points, trust is visible; this is where it's formed, evaluated, measured, and where it can be accelerated.

Contracts are one of these visible points where trust meets action. They are all around us. They bind our world together, and they are part of the natural fabric of any team. They function as a tool for getting people on the same page. They are something to refer to when conflict, uncertainty, or unprecedented issues arise within the relationship.

> *Contracts are the point where*
> *trust meets action.*

Many companies see contracts simply as written documents: letters of agreement, compliance documents, employment contracts, and so on. These are important, of course, but the contracts that underlie an organization are more than documents that we sign. What we're examining here are the tangible interpersonal contracts that bind all teams and form the fabric of societies.

If you look closely, the actions of any group are founded on multiple contracts, which include agreements that are direct and indirect, verbal and nonverbal. These countless agreements between coworkers inform the culture and identity of a team, which affects performance and results. They're often taken for granted; but the communicative network they create reaches every corner of the business. Whether explicit or implicit, these contracts act as silent sources of strength in all organizations. They're the reference points from which trust grows. Without solid explicit and implicit contracts, trust is not possible.

While these kinds of contracts often go overlooked, acknowledging and improving such agreements can have substantial positive effects on your business and your life. Because these contracts are so common—already influencing the organization in ways you might not even realize—this is something you can improve upon without overhauling your operating procedures. This presents a prime opportunity to build trust; simply turning your attention to how these agreements are working for you has the ability to elevate both individuals and teams.

I believe these contracts can be broken down into two primary categories, both of which have the power to increase trust and thus elevate performance.

VERBAL CONTRACTS

Some of the most important contracts in a high-performance organization are spoken ones. These vocalized contracts are a promise that naturally increases accountability. It moves accountability to personal responsibility. On the Blue Angels, as we examined the new landscape of each air show during the brief, we were voicing explicit contracts to each other all the time: "I'm going to be on time and on flight line, the exact moment when the Boss makes the call."

Vocalized contracts are a promise that naturally increases accountability. It moves accountability to personal responsibility.

These kinds of contracts are not superfluous; they allowed us to maintain the standards of safety and performance we were committed to. Elite performers know their words carry not just meaning, but weight. There is a power in their words, which inspires excellence. The Blue Angels are a joking crew, no question, but we are very conscious of the role we've been given and the integrity hanging on our words. When it matters most, we make contracts with one another that allow us to reach for higher and higher levels of execution.

Explicit verbal contracts exist in every business and every team. "I'll get it to you on time" and "I'll follow up with you tomorrow" are verbal contracts—by saying them, it increases and clarifies my accountability. I'm increasing my commitment to get it done. My commitment is made public, and my fulfilling that contract reinforces trust in me. Each fulfillment implies and increases future reliability; each contract fulfilled builds trust between individuals. By making and fulfilling contracts in this way, trust begins to grow. Strong communication builds a cadence where trust can flourish. As I mentioned before, small things matter. As Mother Teresa said, "Be faithful in small things because it is in them that your strength lies."

Strong communication builds a cadence where trust can flourish.

That's a basic example, but it relates to the higher levels of trust. The mechanism doesn't change when the contracts get deeper. "I'll do whatever it takes" or "You can count on me" or "I've got your back"—these are statements that gain incredible power when they are backed by trust. In business we often make a contract to ourselves like "We'll put the client's interest first."

While this kind of goal is often implied, when it is explicit and bought into by both parties, it becomes the foundation that gets you through tough times and also speeds up execution.

As you can see, these kinds of contracts are very different from the standard written kind. Rather than being fail-safes against broken trust, they are inviting trust to be strengthened. They are offering something, creating an environment where trust can grow. This is what makes them so powerful. Each time these contracts are fulfilled, they reinforce the entire team's bond of trust. They create a stronger framework for other team members to offer similar contracts of their own. They are a pillar of the culture and the essence of elite companies.

NONVERBAL CONTRACTS

Implicit, unspoken contracts represent the next level of trust. On a team like the Blues, we made explicit verbal contracts with the team in every brief—to be on time and on flight line—but we also operated on a deep-rooted set of contracts that were rarely verbalized. Our standards were incredibly high, and they functioned as a kind of silent agreement between teammates. The standards of the Blues were familiar to us; we had devoted our lives to upholding them. Their specificity was all around us, because we knew that small things done consistently would result in a greater impact.

Our standards were incredibly high, and they functioned as a kind of silent agreement between teammates.

For example, when we suited up we always carried two types of pens—one for signing autographs, and one for taking notes. We kept them tucked into the upper-left shoulder pocket of our flight suit in a precise order, with the note-taking pen first and the pen for autographs second. We maintained that kind of meticulous precision in all elements of our uniform and in all of our actions. As soon as we left the briefing room, we were 100% polished.

Upholding all the small elements of these standards was so important we created an interesting way to enforce them. Sometimes you would make a mistake and some part of your uniform was out of parameters. If that happened, and you noticed, it was your responsibility to bring it up in the debrief. We gave everyone the opportunity to notice it first themselves, but sometimes it was fun if someone else noticed and it still came up in the debrief. Each time this happened, it incurred a five-dollar fine. We took that money and used it to help pay for our wrap party at the end of the season. It never amounted to much because we corrected our mistakes pretty quickly, but it did raise our awareness and brought some joy to the process. It wasn't about the money, of course; it was about focusing our minds on precision, every single day.

Nonverbal contracts are often visible in teams with a strong strategic CenterPoint. On the Blues, upholding our higher purpose to be ambassadors of goodwill meant that we always showed up prepared and energized, whether for a flight or for a presentation for high school students. We never arrived at any event and said, "Today we're going to be ambassadors of goodwill." We had all made that contract at a deeper, unspoken level. We knew that we represented not only the armed forces, but also the hopes and dreams of all the citizens of the United States and the world at large. A purpose larger than self allowed us to easily buy into and uphold the values and traditions that came before us. Those values still exist on the team today and continue to be passed down to the future. This is the mark of an excellent culture.

TRUST, CONTRACTS, AND THE DPF

Now that you have a clearer picture of how trust and contracts are related, let's contextualize this practice within a process. Contracts are a crucial step in the cycle of the Diamond Performance Framework. Contracts are a point of commitment and buy-in that doesn't live in isolation; it is a living, breathing part of the DPF.

Every brief should leave a team with a set of verbal and nonverbal contracts, commitments that set expectations and can be examined as a larger part of the process.

These commitments can be made at any time, but they flow naturally when the team is gathered for the brief. These commitments will be addressed during the debrief to determine where we fell short of expectations, where we exceeded them, and where the commitments themselves could have been stronger. When the process resets, these commitments pass through the step of elevating beliefs, allowing individuals to enter the

DIAMOND PERFORMANCE FRAMEWORK

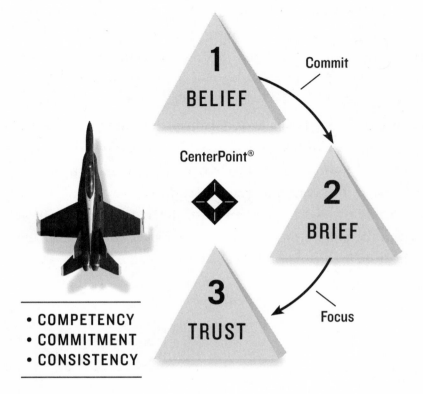

brief with new expectations and trust, forming stronger bonds that can again be debriefed and, as the cycle continues, create an upward spiral of continuous improvement.

When you bring awareness to the power of these contracts, they can be made and engaged with throughout the day. As awareness grows, individuals begin to see this vehicle as a way to increase communication. In this mindset, it's worth that quick phone call, or a text, or popping into someone's office to solidify communication and thus to build trust. In the same way that writing something down can increase the likelihood that we'll remember it, vocalizing our intentions can make us more likely to execute on our actions.

When you're practicing this at the highest levels, you eventually reach a point where people understand expectations and actions without speaking. By applying these techniques, Thumper and I got to the state where we needed very little radio communication. That's how much we trusted one another. We knew what the other person would do and how they would react in a given situation. Your working relationship becomes nonverbal, but you understand it concretely. When you reach predictability—when you can trust, inherently, without thinking, in the actions and character of yourself and those around you—true high performance becomes possible.

7

Culture:
Connection and Extension

*"Culture is simply a shared way of doing
something with a passion."*

—Brian Chesky, Cofounder & CEO, Airbnb

The Blue Angels are one of the oldest flight demonstration squadrons in the world. The team is known for their daring maneuvers, but it's their culture of excellence that makes everything possible. The culture has consistently driven teams to success for decades, since the inception of the Blues in the 1940s. From the beginning, the story of the Blues has been one of passion and commitment.

This story begins in 1946. The Navy was at a crossroads after WWII. Naval aviators' contributions to the war effort had inspired countless newsreels and eye-catching headlines that led to enormous support from the public. But with the close of the war, the Navy saw problems on the horizon. As the world adjusted to times of peace, the public eye shifted its focus. Without media attention, the Navy faced a sharp decline in the number of skilled pilots it could attract. The problem was that building an elite pilot takes years, so if the Navy ran into a talent drought in a time of great need (such as a war), they'd be left without enough pilots to fill essential roles. Leadership needed to find a way to remind people of the boldness and importance of naval aviation, and to inspire and encourage the next generation of leaders.

Admiral Chester Nimitz had a vision for how the Navy could address this problem. His vision would eventually become the world's greatest flight demonstration squadron. Nimitz tasked one of the Navy's finest fighter pilots, Lieutenant Commander Butch Voris, to assemble an elite team and create a program of aerial maneuvers that they could take on the road. The show needed to be amazing: something that would inspire awe in every citizen and show the country the dazzling nature of naval aviation.

Butch, who was a combat ace, was the right man for the job. He put together a small team of the best pilots in the US Navy. They assembled in Jacksonville, Florida, and began creating an aviation experience unlike any other. After countless hours of practice, they had a show. Butch summoned the leadership to the air base in order to demonstrate their creation. The admiral stood by the hangar and watched while the pilots took to the skies in their WWII-era prop planes, the Grumman F6F Hellcat.

The show had the main elements of daring, precision, and

excellence that the team would one day be known for. They flew a three-plane formation in a way that simply hadn't been done before. They brought the thrill of fighter aviation—which happens at high altitude—and brought it low to the ground where the crowd could see the action.

Their greatest challenge was finding a way to fly precision aerobatics without the margin of safety provided by a higher altitude. When they finished the program, they landed and walked over to the admiral, who was shaking his head. As Butch recalled later in an interview, the admiral said to the team, "You're all crazy sons of bitches . . . but it's a great show!"

The team took the show on the road and performed at air bases around the country. The public response was immediate: they were a hit! The crowds were electrified, the Navy was back in the headlines, and it looked as if their mission had been accomplished. But when the success came, they realized they still lacked a crucial component: the team didn't have a name.

The Navy ran a contest to come up with the best name. They got hundreds of submissions (the Sky Dancers, the Flying Buccaneers, the Navy Blue Lancers) but nothing quite stuck. One afternoon, Butch was mulling over the names in a hotel room while his right wing, Maurice Wickendoll, was going through the *New Yorker* magazine. They were in New York for the night and they wanted to go out, so Maurice was reading through the section "Goings On About Town" that lists nightlife and events. Something on the page jumped out at him. There was an upcoming event at one of the hottest clubs in the city, the Blue Angel nightclub, and he said, "Boss, I've got it. The Blue Angels!" The name stuck immediately, and from that moment, the Blue Angels began their long history of excellence.

It's a little bit ironic that the Blue Angels were named after a bar—perfect for Naval aviators![15]

I can imagine the experience those first crowds must have had. When I was flying in those air shows myself, I still thought back to what I felt when I was a kid, the first time I saw the Blues fly. The jets were impressive, but I was also impacted by the sight of their blue flight suits and the sun glinting off their gold helmets. There was something about the interplay between the pilots as they crossed the tarmac to greet the fans that felt special to me. These were the best of the best, and you could sense that instinctively. I felt something stir at the core of my being. I understood that what they did was greater than the cool factor of their coordinated suits or high-tech aircraft. At the time, though, I was 12 years old, and the only word I had for it was "awesome."

Many years later, after I'd learned the skills needed to land a jet on an aircraft carrier, my boyhood admiration demanded greater words, more eloquence. Finally, I heard one of my bosses say something that perfectly expressed how I felt about the Blue Angels. He said, "Aviators aspire to that."

He was right—aviators do aspire to achieve the harmony of skill, teamwork, and daring that the Blue Angels represent. But it took flying with the Blues for me to see that it isn't only aviators who aspire to that level. When I interacted with the crowd after shows, I saw the same thing in their eyes that had

---

15 These quotes from Butch were captured by director Rob Stone in the 1993 Blue Angels documentary, *Around the World at the Speed of Sound*. Rob actually traveled with the team and filmed our European tour that included our stop in Moscow. The documentary is a great insight into the trip, and into the history of the team.

been in mine at 12 years old. Young, old, men, women, every race and social class—they all manifested a deep, awed delight when we approached the crowd line to shake their hands and sign their programs.

Of all these people, there might have been only a handful who wanted to fly jets for a living. So what was it that filled their eyes with wonder? It had to be something that transcended aviation, as well as age, gender, and station in life.

Over time, I've come to realize what it is. We all aspire to be a part of something larger than ourselves. We all aspire to be a part of a culture, a team, a society that is working together in seamless precision to the benefit of everyone involved. What the Blue Angels represent to me is the pinnacle of success in that aspiration. I remember the moment this realization hit me. I was Blue Angel #6 and I had just finished my first air show as opposing solo. As I approached the crowd line for the very first time, I saw this little girl jumping up and down at the front of the crowd. When I got closer, I noticed there was something in her eyes. It was the look of hope and dreams. It was probably the same look I had when I was that young.

> *We all aspire to be a part of something larger than ourselves. We all aspire to be a part of a culture, a team, a society that is working together in seamless precision to the benefit of everyone involved.*

We've all experienced magical moments where we realize we're part of something greater than ourselves. In that moment, I realized I was standing on the shoulders of all the giants who came before me. I was the product of all my experience, of all the teachers and mentors I'd had over the years. I realized that I needed to take on a larger purpose and become the best example for others who were trying to achieve their life's ambitions. And most importantly, I had to be selfless. I knew it wasn't about me, it was about the team, the culture, and our shared purpose.

The Blue Angels' gold helmets and blue flight suits were representative of this distinct culture. The helmet is painted a vibrant yellow. It has a reflective gold visor, similar to what NASA uses for astronauts. It allows you to look straight into the sun without squinting. The last thing you want is to be flying 36 inches away from someone and have the sun get in your eyes. No other aviators in the armed forces wear the gold helmet. The helmets are reserved for members of the Blues. It's something you have to earn. It represents 1/10 of 1/10 of 1% of all jet pilots. It is the icon of our quest for high performance and continuous improvement, our commitment to each other and to the team. Being allowed to wear the gold helmet is a tremendous honor.

Sometimes I see the same look in people's eyes today when they see my gold helmet that I bring with me to speaking engagements. People at my events are rarely hopeful pilots or even aviation enthusiasts. They are leaders, employees, and parents with dreams and goals that are highly specific. I see the range of aspirations that inhabit any given room when I meet people after my talks. For many of them the gold helmet is a symbol for raising their beliefs and reaching beyond. They want to get close to it, to see their own faces mirrored in its visor. I usually hand it to them so we can take a photo together, and give a fighter-pilot thumbs-up.

The reason the helmet inspires awe is that it's an icon of a culture of excellence, and a culture of caring. Icons are one way to help people sustain shared values and beliefs. Tangible things like that gold helmet serve as powerful reminders of our potential, and that potential is nothing without the belief that we can do something with it. Icons allow us to access this belief in a way that almost nothing else can. They allow us to envision ourselves as we aspire to be. Understanding the elements that our unique culture was built from can help activate this same system of values and actions in any team.

THE CULTURE OF THE GOLD HELMET

A team's culture is what sets it apart. And the culture of a team has a major impact on results. Great teams are built from great individuals; but on elite teams, the whole is greater than the sum of its parts.

The culture of the Blue Angels is distinct because it lasts well beyond any individual's career with the Blues. I remember the day I had a chance to finally meet Butch Voris. He told me that in his day, in the late 1940s, the Blue Angels represented the best of the best, but today's team is better than they ever were, and next year's team is going to be even better than the team this year. That humility gets passed down to newbies along with the tradition of high performance.

As the torchbearer to this tradition, it's your job not only to uphold it but also to make it better. The transmission of methods and mindset from one team to the next is what allows the Blue Angels to perform at the highest levels year in and year out. While the personnel change, the culture endures. The key to creating a successful elite team is building a successful culture. A strong culture takes individual attributes, talents, and interests and creates something greater.

Our cohesion on the Blues came in part from our shared experience of an extreme situation, but it went well beyond that. When your life is on the line, and more importantly when someone else's life depends on you, you don't want to let them down. Although our environment was unique, the same holds true for any team or business. Creating strong bonds requires work, both professionally and personally.

The key to creating a successful elite team is building a successful culture. A strong culture takes individual attributes, talents, and interests and creates something greater.

For us, our environment provided a unique opportunity to share and build our culture. To fly without a G-suit, as we did on the Blues, requires a lot of physical strength. Fighting against sustained G's isn't easy; you have to squeeze your legs, your stomach, and every ounce of your body, forcing the blood back into your head as gravity tries to pull it away. The best way to increase your G tolerance is with physical strength. In the three years I served on the team, part of our daily routine was working out with heavy weights. It was something we did *together* that helped us build chemistry. It was part of our job that was built into the way we trained. Around 5:00 PM, following our afternoon flight and debrief, we would get together and hit the gym for about two hours.

This ritual was especially important during winter training, when we would take the new team from Pensacola, Florida, to El Centro, California. Being in a remote location removed distractions and allowed us the space we needed to fully commit to our mission ahead. Because new pilots and personnel come in every year, the team needs to be socialized—to rebuild the chemistry we need to execute the best air show possible. As new members come in, the culture stays, but the chemistry changes. Each team is unique and takes on its own personality.

As new members come in, the culture stays, but the chemistry changes.

Working out together was a ritual of connection and extension. It's not so distant from what I see happening all the time at business conferences. Anyone who's spent time at an event like this knows that at the core, these events are planned to bring alignment, commitment, and most important, to connect people. The goal is connection. A lot of learning comes from that shared experience, and it's not just the workshops and planned networking sessions. There are human interactions going on all over the place as people connect and get to know one another.

The Blues—like many other high-performing teams and companies—are built on a culture of learning. Everything is framed by a caring, sharing, and mentoring mindset. Caring and sharing is a form of mentorship that is special. It's not obligatory; it comes from the heart. That's what it feels like in a Blue Angel brief or debrief.

Mentorship is the mechanism we use to transfer that spirit of caring and sharing. I would never be where I am today if it weren't for those who taught me—whether it was specific tactics, or opening doors for me. That's something I experienced in the Navy generally, but it was even more obvious among the Blue Angels. There's a subtlety to the way the Blues fly that cannot be learned in a classroom. You can't sit down with books or lectures and teach someone how to be a successful Blue Angel pilot. It has to be learned with the stick in your hand, repeating every action countless times until you've mastered it. That mastery is personal, but it can be transmitted. On a team like the Blues, you'll never reach mastery if you can't learn from the experience of others.

That's why the Blues have created a system where every incoming pilot is matched up with a current veteran who becomes their mentor. The veteran pilot has only been there one year longer, but that's enough for them to pass on knowledge and wisdom as you are trying to achieve a dramatic improvement in skills. At this level, one year is equivalent to a lifetime in an average setting. The knowledge is deep but the risk is high. You have to step up your game. Their job as a mentor is both training the techniques and passing on the culture. It's how you fly *and* how you behave.

You'll never reach mastery if you can't learn from the experience of others.

Once you know what position you're going to fly, you know who your mentor is going to be. For incoming diamond pilots (positions #2 and #3), your mentor is #4, the slot pilot. For #6, the incoming solo, your mentor is #5, the lead solo pilot. The interesting thing is that you have one year as a trainee; by the following year, you take on your own mentor's position, serving as the source of knowledge for incoming pilots. The transition happens quickly, and requires a structure and a mindset. The position of the Boss is unique in this setup. As the flight leader in the formation, he is coached by #2, his right wingman, and #4, the slot pilot. The Boss also has a special relationship with #5, the lead solo and operations officer. This is typically a third-year person on the team, one who has the most experience in the air show environment as well as the cultural and strategic priorities of the team.

In business, rarely does the transition go this fast. That's good, because a decrease in turnover brings continuity. But there's still something to be learned from the way we did it on the Blues. I often see people in business who are guarded and afraid of losing their jobs, and therefore withhold information that could be valuable to another person. On the Blues it was just the opposite; we knew we were going to move on. In fact, it was our duty to make the people who came after us as good or better than we were the year before. There were no withholds and no surprises. We took everything we had and laid it on the table. I bring this up to point out how different this perspective is from that of many organizations; clearly this allowed us to develop and grow everyone around us without fear. A culture of caring and sharing is only possible when these kinds of fears are driven out.

A culture of mentorship is one of learning and caring. Teams that focus on these ideas create positive growth. Teams that aren't focused on learning and development can become stagnant, having a direct and negative impact on results. Every single day of the show season, no matter how successful our flight had been, we came into every brief and debrief with a focus on improvement. Getting better meant that we constantly had to learn and develop our skills. Having veteran pilots around to mentor us also represented a level of expertise that exceeded anything I'd experienced before.

These are the pillars of a strong high-performance culture. And while it's clear how mentorship can have an impact on a relatively small, tight-knit team like the Blue Angels, it also works—and is especially effective—in a larger arena.

TAKING MENTORSHIP ACROSS THE ORGANIZATION

The process of mentorship is at the heart of one of the most successful widespread programs in naval history: the United States Navy Fighter Weapons School, more commonly referred to as TOPGUN. I didn't attend the school myself, but I've flown with them in exercises and have benefited from working closely with graduates, absorbing the unique discipline and focus of their training. Also, as I mentioned, my connection with the school feels a little deeper, having done some of the flying for the Hollywood movie *Top Gun*.

TOPGUN began as a response to a problem. In 1968, the US military was losing an unprecedented number of aircraft in the air war in Vietnam. To put it in perspective, during WWII, the win/loss ratio in air-to-air combat was around 10:1, which means that for every aircraft the United States lost, we shot down 10 of the enemy. In 1968, an investigation revealed that during the preceding years in Vietnam, that number had fallen to 2.5:1, a devastating statistic from the US point of view.

The need for change was clear and immediate, for both the Air Force and the Navy, but the cause of the decreased ratio was up for debate. How the Navy interpreted these numbers is what makes this an interesting story.

Both organizations had the same question in mind: How do you give the average pilot a better-than-average chance of survival? After analyzing the data, the majority of leadership attributed the problem to a technological failing, concluding that US aircraft were too vulnerable to an attack from the rear. Both the Air Force and the Navy responded by upgrading their aircraft to be less susceptible to that kind of attack, and instituted technical advancements like enhanced radar capabilities and upgraded missile technology. This move was in line with the prevailing view about air-to-air combat at the time.

The dominant aircraft of the era, the F-4 Phantom, is a case in point. Its advanced radar technology and missile systems were designed to eliminate the need to merge with enemy fighters, a practice more commonly known as dogfighting. The thought was that by keeping distance between fighters, they could eliminate the need for direct engagement.

While both the Navy and the Air Force had similar conclusions about their aircraft, the Navy spent less time focusing on technical enhancements, and instead focused their efforts in a different area. This was all thanks to the insight of one now-legendary officer, Captain Frank Ault. He published his analysis of the situation in *The Ault Report*, more formally known as the *Air-to-Air Missile System Capability Review*.

The *Ault Report* took a contrarian view. After analyzing the data, Captain Ault attributed the decline in win/loss ratio to inadequate Air Combat Maneuvering, or ACM. The report called for an increase in air combat training as a solution and made specific suggestions that led directly to the founding of the Navy Fighter Weapons School. Instead of trying to eliminate dogfighting, the *Ault Report* took the problems of dogfighting head on and called for a complete overhaul of the way the Navy approached ACM.

TOPGUN revolutionized the entire system of Navy fighter training. At the heart of this transformation was a huge shift in culture. Previously, air-to-air debriefs were dominated by the loudest or most senior voice in the room. The first one to the chalkboard with the most aggressive style called all the shots. But in TOPGUN, as laid out in the *Ault Report*, everyone in the debrief was valued and allowed to contribute. They depersonalized their critiques and opened each other up to learn from their mistakes. Pilots in TOPGUN no longer felt like they had to defend themselves during a debrief. In this new environment, not only could they share the wisdom of their failures, it also became imperative that they do just that. They took their shields down, opened up their notebooks, and began to engage with a new process of learning and improvement.

It looked good on paper, but no one knew the value of this approach until the program started. In 1969, TOPGUN trained its first students. The school started small, operating out of a trailer at the Naval Air Station in Miramar, California.

TOPGUN aviators were selected for their skill, pedigree, and leadership potential. These pilots were trained extensively in air combat maneuvering. The rules of engagement were completely rewritten, allowing for more freedom during flight and allowing pilots the ability to push the aircraft and work together in close contact in a way that was simply not allowed before.

The task of retraining every fighter pilot in the fleet would have been impossible, and with the immediacy of the war in Vietnam, simply training incoming pilots and waiting for the new culture to take over was not an option. Instead, on the suggestion of Captain Ault, they adopted a basic "train the trainer" model: each TOPGUN graduate would take the knowledge and skills they learned, go back to the fleet, and share it with their squadrons. With graduates throughout the fleet, the knowledge could disseminate throughout the entire organization, quickly.

By the time the aerial missions over North Vietnam resumed in 1972, there was a TOPGUN graduate in nearly every squadron in the Navy. The Air Force, which had focused their campaign on technical improvements, saw an initial decrease in its win/loss ratio. The Navy, however, saw an incredible increase, hitting a ratio of 12.5/1, a 25% increase from the high in WWII. The results immediately validated the Fighter Weapons School approach, beginning a legacy of elite excellence that continues to this day. The Air Force quickly followed suit, setting up its own fighter weapons school focused on elevating ACM training.

I love sharing this story with businesses because it illustrates the kind of actions that make successful teams unique. At the end of the day, great teams are the product of the people on them, and how those people interact with one another. That's what makes the culture of the team. The history of

TOPGUN shows us the kind of improvement that a cultural shift can bring. Great teams are not defined by the technology and tools they have at their disposal. That part is important, but it's not sufficient on its own. Teams that excel are defined by attributes like chemistry, trust, openness, and a culture of sharing. I've seen this firsthand, both as a Blue Angel and in my time working with some of the world's largest, most successful companies.

Great teams are not defined by technology and tools but by chemistry, trust, openness, and a culture of sharing.

Investing time and energy in creating a strong culture with well-defined standards and expectations is critical. Strong culture has the power to elevate every action and every interaction in an organization of any size. For those who understand the importance of culture, there is a significant opportunity to elevate results in a way that is repeatable and scalable. On the other side of the coin, the failure of company culture can have the same far-reaching effects, causing diminished results. Culture matters. Culture is king. It's a long-term differentiator that allows one not only to adapt to change, but to lead through change.

8

Glad To Be Here Debrief:
Secret Sauce

"An organization's ability to learn, and translate that learning into action rapidly, is the ultimate competitive advantage."

—Jack Welch, Former CEO, General Electric

As you've learned in previous chapters, the Blues put extreme emphasis on preparation and focus—all of which come before the show. But the real power of the Blue Angels, and of any high-performance team, is the ability to learn and adapt quickly. There is a special tool available to every individual and team on the planet that will help you achieve this goal. I call it the Glad To Be Here Debrief.

This tool can, by itself, establish a mindset and culture of improvement. It's something elite teams know well; and we used it every single day that I was a Blue Angel. The debrief may seem familiar at first glance, but when practiced in the way that I'm going to describe, it becomes one of the biggest opportunities to elevate individual and team performance. This is the key, final step in the Diamond Performance Framework. It's where you take everything that you created in the previous steps (Beliefs, Brief, CenterPoint, Trust) and imbue it with a process focused on continuous improvement. The debrief was a mechanism that tuned our minds and made every action a step toward improvement. It came toward the end of our day, but it was actually the beginning of our next performance. It was part of our daily process. It wasn't something we reached for when things went wrong. We did it every time we flew. It was built into the culture and DNA of the organization.

In business, there is often a negative bias associated with having a debrief. I believe this is because most individuals and organizations debrief only when there is a mistake, a negative outcome, or a fault to find. I've seen this in companies around the world. This fear-based approach is the opposite of what we were doing on the Blue Angels. On the contrary, our goal was to drive fear out of the organization. That's why we created a safe environment in the debrief where we could all open up and share the wisdom of our success and our failure, side by side. Furthermore, we used these gatherings to cultivate positive interpersonal dynamics within the team. This is about far more than the analysis of root causes. Debriefing in this way instills chemistry and camaraderie in the team. It provides leadership opportunities for everyone on the team. It gives people the chance to reinforce the positive and raise expectations. It's more than a team-building process; it's a team-building *mindset*.

Many might wonder, "If you had a great performance, what need is there to deconstruct it?" That's the key question here. If organizations can change this negative mindset and implement a process that works, it can be a huge game-changer. In sports and business, debriefing sessions have led to wins and increased bottom lines; but the benefits are bigger than that. In the right setting, this tool has the power to save lives. On the Blues, the extreme environment we lived in demanded it. In healthcare, in society, when lives are on the line, this is what you need to create elevated execution.

It may seem counterintuitive to examine your victories alongside your failures, but by focusing only on the negative aspects of performance, you are ignoring some of the most valuable information. This is a huge misconception about a debrief: that it serves only to examine your failures. With those kinds of associations, it's not surprising that so few people take the time to do it. In our Blue Angel debriefs, we examined the good and the bad together. We even called them "goods and others." That distinction points to the overall positivity of this approach. We focused on the aspects of what went well so we could continue to improve. When we shared areas where we were out of parameters, we made contracts to adjust our actions in the future. By laying our shortcomings on the table in this way, we employed the wisdom of the entire team to confront challenges as they arose.

In addition to realigning our actions, the debrief was a place where we acted out the interpersonal dynamics that made us such a special team. These specific standards of bearing defined the way we treated one another and how we interacted as a team. This made the debrief far more than a meeting; it was a transcendent experience that gave us an identity and played a major part in our success. It empowered accountability to become personal responsibility, and with personal responsibility, accountability became a given.

*The debrief was far more than a meeting;
it was a transcendent experience that
gave us an identity and played a major
part in our success.*

What makes a Glad To Be Here debrief different is the uniquely safe environment. This can be achieved when the perspective is shifted from negative review to positive growth. The sole purpose of a Glad To Be Here debrief is to achieve continuous improvement by elevating and sharing information that draws on everyone's experience. Everyone's participation is important, which is what makes having a safe environment so critical. The end goal is to take all available information and bring it into the next cycle.

When you start to debrief in this way, the whole experience is imbued with a grateful mindset. This is how the highest performers approach the world, in business and in life. A debrief without gratitude is actually a negatively focused exercise. You're looking at what you can fix, but only from a negative perspective. While that component is good and can be useful, if it's all you do, over time, you start to beat yourself up. In that situation, the process of improvement becomes a source of stress as opposed to a source of excitement and focus. The Glad To Be Here mindset changes everything for a team. In this state of mind, you can talk about things that need to be fixed through shared beliefs and with a higher sense of purpose. This gives everyone the ability and energy to be more resilient.

INSIDE A BLUE ANGEL DEBRIEF

At the end of a Blue Angel air show, all six jets buzz the crowd in delta formation, blowing smoke over the cheering fans before we pitch up one last time for landing. This is the final maneuver of the day, but we like to say that the show isn't over until we've taxied the jets in front of the crowd and the wheels are in the chocks.

From the moment my wheels touched the runway, and I decelerated on the rollout, my mind went from a super-high state of focus and back into a "normal" state. This always felt like a natural moment of relaxation—as if you were letting out a big sigh. It was a moment to be grateful to have had that incredible experience. But I never got to completely relax because the day was far from over. As we taxied into the chocks—all six jets parked in perfect unison before the crowd—I ran through my checklist and loosened the heavy straps that held me down in the seat while I flew upside down. On the Boss's signal, we opened our canopies in perfect unison. As the fresh air blew into the cockpit, I heard the crowd cheering for the first time. I stepped out on the ladder and saw them waving from behind a rope at the crowd line. As I entered the scene, going from the extremes of the flight to the joy of the crowd, I felt like I was coming out of a cocoon and into the world.

I climbed down the ladder and found my crew chief standing at attention in front of the jet. We shook hands and gave each other a knowing look. This was how we acknowledged the special bond between us; words were rarely spoken or needed. We did the same after every show. The bond we shared was like professional athletes in an arena; we were focused on each other, even though we were surrounded by thousands of fans.

After a quick exchange with our maintenance supervisors, we went to the crowd line. This was always my favorite part of the air show. It was the moment we embraced the public and engaged in our mission to inspire and serve as ambassadors of goodwill. I loved meeting the kids and their families, getting a chance to shake their hands and talk to them. When you see these magnificent planes doing magical things, it's easy to forget there's actually a human in that airplane, flying with stick and throttle, just like back in the days of early flight. Putting a face with the jet gives people a sense that what we're doing is distinctly human and magical at the same time. It contributes to the awe factor.

To anyone watching an air show, this might seem like the end of our day. The cars that filled the massive parking areas start to snake away, the planes are refueled and buttoned up, and everything has an air of winding down. But in truth, this was the most important part of our day. We transitioned from being in public and returned back to our inner sanctum, back to the same conference room where we had conducted our pre-flight brief. The sign is still on the door, "Blue Angels Only," and as soon as we enter, the atmosphere changes. This is the beginning of a Glad To Be Here Debrief.

When you first walk in, you can immediately sense whether it was a good or a challenging show. Either way, we get down to business very quickly. A hush gradually falls over the room. The room becomes dead quiet, as each pilot turns inward, collecting their thoughts. You can see people writing notes on their picture of the show site preparing their thoughts and comments about what just happened. You can tell that we are about to do something we all take very seriously. In this moment, everyone is locked and loaded and the debrief begins.

DEBRIEF CADENCE

There are many ways to implement a debrief process. Time is the first challenge that comes up. Perhaps the main opponents to this type of **debrief** are those who think there isn't enough time. In my experience, this can be easily overcome. Once you've gone through the experience, you begin to understand the ability of this practice to change the way your team interacts. That said, if time is a major issue, the process can be adapted to fit different time constraints. There are many opportunities, large and small, where an exchange of information will contribute to future success.

I like to break debriefs down into three types. The first one is a **real-time** debrief. It can be as simple as a quick phone call, or stopping someone in the hallway to discuss something that happened. This is quick and powerful. It takes into account the same perspective and components that I've described above and condenses them down into an instant. In this mindset, unexpected moments become an opportunity to debrief and share information.

Another type of debrief is a **periodic debrief**. This is perhaps the most common. A periodic debrief is based on regular intervals of time, and could occur weekly, monthly, or even quarterly. These regular intervals are used to inform and to update, while simultaneously focusing on improvement. Whether it's daily for teams that interact that often, or quarterly for larger departmental actions, periodic debriefs are one of the most common types.

Another kind of debrief is marked by occurrences; I like to think of it as a **post-event debrief**. The Blue Angels do this after every air show. This can also happen after a sales meeting or after a large conference. The key is to hold it immediately afterward, or as close to the event as possible. Fast feedback is strong feedback. By examining an event from all angles, from multiple perspectives, you uncover valuable information that can inform how you plan and act in future events.

> *Fast feedback is strong feedback.*

Once you understand where and when a debrief like this can take place, you need to adopt a basic structure and apply it to those moments. What follows is a framework I've created that mimics what we were doing and achieving when I was a Blue Angel. Within this framework, different teams will employ slightly different approaches; but it's important to have a basic sense of what's going to happen, such as who is going to speak, and when.

At a high level, there are two basic components that create the cadence: the General-Safe and Specifics. Think of each part as a sequence. In each one, participants get the opportunity to comment on the subject being discussed. Participants come into the debrief ready to deliver a General-Safe, and then to discuss their personal Specifics.

PART ONE: THE GENERAL-SAFE

A General-Safe is a simple statement that serves as a point of entry into the debrief, where each participant takes a turn making a brief statement. It gets its name from what it contains: a general overview, and also any "safeties"[16] you might have to share. This round gives the team a sense of the collective mood, and allows for quick input and exchanges that might detract from the next section, focused on Specifics.

Sometimes it's important for a leader to go first and set the tone; at other times, a leader should go last, so as not to influence the opening comments. Regardless of the order, the debrief will give each individual the opportunity to make opening comments about their experiences during the event being discussed. These comments are an overview that gives the team insight into the mindset of the person who is delivering them. This General-Safe round aligns the team's focus on the subject at hand and sets the tone for the entire meeting. It is an opportunity to reveal key information about yourself that might help the team, as well as acknowledge and reinforce others. Since the round of specifics is upcoming, these comments should be short and to the point.

The opening comments of the debrief set the tone and can strengthen or detract from the entire engagement. For that reason, the General-Safe allows for multiple levels of input in a short space of time. Here are four basic components of a strong General-Safe:

I. Feeling statement: This is a chance for each individual to give a quick general overview of the event or subject that focuses on their personal feelings. This opens you up to the team, giving them an insight into your mindset,

---

16 A safety is an error committed that was outside of standard operating procedures or a variance in your performance that needs to be addressed.

and how you're thinking at the moment. Be open, honest, and transparent.

2. Safety and "I'll fix it": Every team needs standards that define their performance. In the brief, you need to know those standards, because in the debrief, we determine where we've strayed from those standards. A safety is a variance that did have—or more importantly *could* have had—a big impact. It's an opportunity to show the team you were out of parameters. Be the first to acknowledge your own mistakes—without fear—and address them with an "I'll fix it" statement that shows the team your awareness and commitment. By saying this, it doesn't mean that you'll never make a mistake again, but it shows that you are aware of the parameters, and you're taking corrective action. This builds trust and inspires personal responsibility.

3. Acknowledgments: This is where participants address what went well. Give credit and praise to individuals who have done well, or speak of something you want to reinforce. This is about sharing praise in a public setting. A simple "thank you" can be very powerful.

4. "Glad To Be Here": End your General-Safe with these four words, every time. They signal that you are finished and move focus to the next person; but they do far more than that. The brain learns from repetition. The more you say these words, the more real they become. This statement reaffirms your commitment to the team, and over time, it can remind you of your purpose larger than self.

It's an acknowledgment for your thankfulness to have the opportunities and challenges that life presents. While emotions vary day to day, the intent is to stay aligned on a positive mindset.

5. "Oh, by the way" (optional): After everyone has had the opportunity to give a General-Safe, open the floor to any reinforcing or additional comments that were triggered as a result of the participants' statements. Sometimes the round of General-Safe uncovers small things that can be addressed with an "Oh, by the way . . ."

As your debrief practice develops, these steps will flow seamlessly and create the groundwork you need to get at the core issues. Try to keep comments both quick and genuine.

PART TWO: SPECIFICS

After everyone has had the opportunity for General-Safe, it's time to get into Specifics. If the General-Safe is the spark that ignites the team and sets the appropriate mood, then Specifics are the engine that drives the airplane. The General-Safe is adaptable depending on the size and scope of the debrief. The Specifics, however, will grow from the nature of the subject.

This is where the debrief opens up. Each individual goes through the checklist or notes they have prepared. The team will have the opportunity to respond, debate, and contribute to every point. Specifics should address what went well, what didn't go well, and what could be improved.

This is the meat of the debrief, and as such, the contours will vary from team to team, and from subject to subject. The subject is not what defines this practice. What makes a Glad To Be Here Debrief different is the perspective. It's not what you're talking about, but how you're talking about it. Years after I left the Blues, I began to analyze the keys of our success, and I realized that all of our gatherings were defined by specific interpersonal dynamics.

That's why we kept the sign on the door and treated the room as our inner sanctum. These intimate approaches to human interaction are the key to getting the most from your Specifics, and unleashing exponential results.

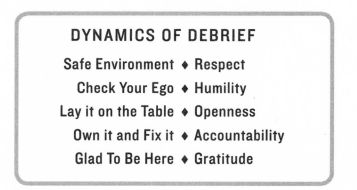

DYNAMICS OF DEBRIEF

Here are the dynamics that define the process, and allow you to turn a debrief into a tool for continuous improvement.

SAFE ENVIRONMENT = RESPECT

This dynamic is crucial for optimizing communication. In a safe environment, each individual perspective unites to create the clearest picture of what went well and what didn't. Without this dynamic, individuals can withhold information out of fear, which creates blind spots that can inhibit improvement.

In a Glad To Be Here debrief, every member of the team—regardless of experience or position—is deeply valued and should have the respect of everyone participating. In the presence of respect, all ideas are liberated and allowed to enter the discussion. Lack of respect can lead to crippling fear—fear of speaking out or fear of failure.

A safe environment is critical; without it, important ideas can go unsaid. Even the smallest comment can trigger a conversation that ends up solving a major issue.

> *A safe environment is critical; without it, important ideas can go unsaid.*

In the debriefing room, there is a shared responsibility for the tone and the outcome. Every participant has the power to make the room a safe, positive space where everyone gathers to improve. A safe environment is not a given. Leadership matters, but ultimately this dynamic is something that a team builds together over time. Once established in this way, it has the power to improve every interaction, both inside and outside the debriefing room.

CHECK YOUR EGO = HUMILITY

Elite teams are made up of high-performing individuals, but not all high-performing individuals are able to come together and form an elite team. Individual talent fuels team performance, but letting your ego take over in the debrief will always have a negative effect. High performers have egos, but the difference is that we're all in it together. There's a need for humility. You have to acknowledge who's in the room, and give a clear sense of roles, but you want to be able to level the playing field. There's still a respect for others' positions, but in a Glad To Be Here Debrief, rank is laid on the table in the spirit of team results. There's still respect for others' positions, however. It's a balance. When ego, rank, and status are left at the door, the debrief becomes an open environment, fueling an atmosphere of psychological safety and openness that is necessary for optimum results. A productive debrief requires a spirit of humility and selflessness. There is strength in vulnerability.

When the second dynamic—Check Your Ego—becomes a reality in your debrief, the outcome is personal humility. Efforts become unified, and the team takes on a strong character and reputation of its own—one that is focused on a purpose larger than self.

By checking your ego at the door, you are basically saying that you are committed to the team over self. And because of this higher commitment, you're going to be someone who is an example of all the attributes the team represents. Removing your ego from the equation supports each of the other dynamics of the Glad To Be Here Debrief. If you are contributing to a safe environment, it has to be with others in mind. If you lay it on the table, you're offering your perspective as a team-learning opportunity. Freedom from ego will allow you to take accountability and cultivate a mindset of grateful generosity.

LAY IT ON THE TABLE = OPENNESS AND HONESTY

Even when the previous dynamics are present, it still takes action to get the most out of the debrief. Lay It on the Table is about action and speaking without fear of criticism or reprimand. Great leaders help their teams align on decisions so that there's buy-in and commitment from everyone, which results in joint accountability for results.

The third dynamic of debrief—Lay It on the Table—conveys a willingness of everyone in the room to suspend hierarchical thinking in the interest of results. This type of openness requires humility, transparency, and fearlessness. That only happens if there's a safe environment of respect. That's when teams can celebrate wins and face difficult challenges in ways that activate excellence.

A climate in which people are capable and willing to Lay It on the Table is a powerful motivator. It allows everyone to shine and step up. They can speak their minds without being bullied or steamrolled.

OWN IT AND FIX IT = ACCOUNTABILITY

The fourth dynamic of debrief—Own It and Fix It—has two parts. When you own something, you're more apt to take good care of it and fix any problems as soon as you see them. You don't wait for someone else to fix it, because you own it. It's your responsibility. High-performing teams are made up of individuals who don't just accept ownership; they *take* it. When you have personal responsibility, accountability is a given.

By owning specific tasks, the results of a project, good or bad, come into play in the actions of the individual. A culture where everyone has skin in the game is one that is far more effective. Sometimes it's the subtleties that take us over the goal line. Ownership means getting it done, whether that means adapting or being proactive.

When you have personal responsibility, accountability is a given.

Own It and Fix It is also a matter of pride. This is true both for the individual and the team. When a team succeeds, every individual on that team succeeds together. Our victories and our failures become common property, and when that becomes true for your team, there is a huge opportunity to increase performance.

GLAD TO BE HERE = GRATITUDE

If a safe environment is the dynamic that makes everything possible, then Glad To Be Here—the fifth and final dynamic—is the game-changer that triggers extreme performance. These four simple words encompass an effective debrief. When people bring a Glad To Be Here mindset to the table, it sets the tone for buy-in and ownership of outcomes. Gratitude is the secret sauce for this kind of continuous improvement. It's the energy that allows you to sustain greatness. This approach to excellence would not be complete without it. It's a simple saying that sets you apart in personal and professional environments.

It changes everything. It allows you to pick up clues and take appropriate action.

With a grateful mindset, teams can easily process negative feedback and turn it into positive results.

A number of studies on the effects of gratitude confirm a correlation between thankfulness and positive results. In one series conducted by the University of Kentucky, gratitude was shown to increase pro-social behaviors and lower aggression in various groups.[17] That's exactly the kind of effect that teams need, especially in an open, honest environment where everything is laid on the table. Gratitude is a social emotion; it binds us together and strengthens our bonds, regardless of the nature of our relationships. With this mindset, teams can more easily process negative feedback and turn it into positive results.

Other studies show astonishing personal benefits to expressing gratitude. In one study that has been emulated many times, University of California psychologists discovered that participants who regularly expressed gratitude reported higher levels of well-being. They exercised more and recorded fewer visits to the doctor.[18] When we are actively grateful, it activates new

---

17 C. Nathan DeWall et al., "A Grateful Heart is a Nonviolent Heart," Sep. 6, 2011, http://journals.sagepub.com/doi/abs/10.1177/1948550611416675.

18 R. A. Emmons et al., "Counting Blessings versus Burdens: An Experimental Investigation of Gratitude and Subjective Well-Being in Daily Life," *Journal of Personality and Social Psychology* (Feb. 2003): Vol. 84, No. 2, 377–89.

DIAMOND PERFORMANCE FRAMEWORK

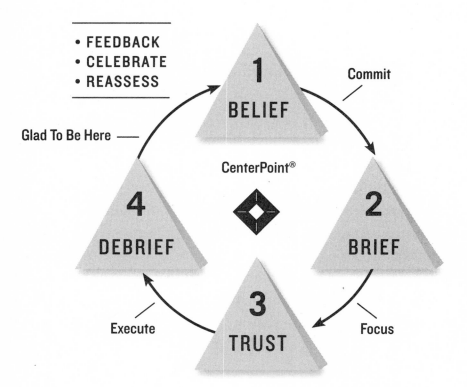

pathways in the mind and changes the way we see and understand the world. A grateful mindset changes our perspective. It helps us spot opportunities, both to help others and to realize our success. It can boost our potential to be creative and innovative. Gratitude changes the game and changes your world.

Applying this mindset to your debrief practice is crucial. It gives you a new perspective on the entire process. As I've said, organizations typically employ a debrief when things go wrong, thus bringing a negative connotation to the process. The Glad To Be Here mindset changes that perspective and reveals opportunity, even amid setbacks. In addition to a fresh perspective, a state of joy and gratitude has a calming effect that stimulates new thoughts and ideas, which might otherwise be lost.

COMING FULL CIRCLE

The Glad To Be Here debrief can only be fully understood within the context of the Diamond Performance Framework. As the last step in this cyclical process, the debrief is key to rebooting the system and kicking off continuous improvement. This is the inflection point where the past and the present come together to create a better future. Nothing creates greater results in the future than an effective debrief. The debrief utilizes everything that has happened in the previous steps and puts it through a structured, positive review. This step is critical to maintaining both the process and the mindset you need to achieve higher performance.

A grateful mindset changes our perspective. It helps us spot opportunities, both to help others and to realize our success.

There's a rhythm to the Diamond Performance Framework. The debrief allows you to reassess and elevate your belief levels, which brings focus to your highest potential. With elevated expectations, the brief allows you to prepare for your best action. Building high trust enables execution with commitment. And finally, the debrief allows you to process all of that information and imbue it with gratitude. This is the flow of high performance. It is a spiraling up process which inspires a state of focused awareness that brings new power each time the process repeats. As the steps become habit, they create a forward pull that makes higher and higher performance possible.

This cycle gives you the structure you need to achieve flow, but that's only the beginning. Eventually, the pursuit of excellence will take you far beyond what you thought was possible into a space beyond high performance where we can engage with our natural state. In this space, it is possible to see the awe in everything, and to experience a life of magic. I know this from experience. There is a place beyond high performance. Let's go there.

9

Beyond High Performance: Glad To Be Here

"Gate, Gate, Paragate, Para sam gate Bodhi svaha."
"Go, go, go beyond the horizon, go completely
beyond the horizon, do it!"

—Heart Sutra

High performance is the beginning of something special. Mastery of the world within you ultimately brings mastery of the world around you. With an elite process and mindset to guide you on this journey, anything is possible. When you stay the course, you'll eventually discover a space beyond high performance where it is possible to live a life of magic. In this space, you live and experience every moment in a state of awe. It's incredible, but it feels natural—and I believe this is actually our natural state. When you live in this way, you see commitment and trust with honor. You're living in the present, constantly learning from the past, and designing the future with joy.

Mastery of the world within you ultimately brings mastery of the world around you.

This space beyond high performance is something that I became aware of slowly, over the course of my life. Whether I was flying, studying in school, or working in business, the pursuit of mastery changed my perspective on everything. As I faced new challenges, I began to notice that my tactical approaches inevitably became more holistic.

Between the Cats and Traps of countless carrier landings, in the space between myself and the jet, I experienced a shift that affected the way I flew and, ultimately, the way I lived my life and saw the world. This change in awareness came no matter what kind of challenge I was facing. It seemed to be a natural part of progressing, and I began to think of it as something that was repeatable and transferable. It was the product of my training, my practice, and all the ways I learned to prepare. It was a feeling of expansion and contraction, connection and extension. That's what happens the moment you go beyond yourself: you feel a beautiful sensation of being connected with the world around you. In moments of action, you feel a focused awareness that flows naturally, even effortlessly. Things happen fast, yet appear slow. I believe this happens because when you are fully prepared and confident in your ability to execute, you become acutely present. That's what I eventually felt when I flew an F-18.

This sensation first came to me somewhere in the middle of my career as a pilot. Once you've spent enough time in a cockpit, you learn a simple lesson: you have to fly the airplane, and not let the airplane fly you. In other words, you have to be proactive, not reactive. There's a capability that comes when you make that distinction, and this gives you calmness and strength. It will also improve your landing grades in a big way!

The thing that changes is this: when you first start flying, there's a duality—man and machine. Your actions are purely tactile. You have checklists and standard operating procedures that tell you *what* to do and *when* to do it. Your actions are guided by a fear of making mistakes. When you're in this stage, you're still behind the airplane. The elements of flight are purely mechanical, literally following the steps laid out in a manual.

For example, every aerobatic maneuver has a script. A barrel roll is built from a series of specific steps. There is a certain entry airspeed, the nose is pulled up to 45 degrees, followed by a left roll to hit a 90-degree off-set, and a recovery at the same airspeed and altitude as your entry. The steps have clear definitions with numbers and ideas that provide a boundary for success. The first time you do these maneuvers, you can feel yourself focusing on those steps; you're simply trying to hit the gates. Everything remains broken down into checkpoints. Actions are fragmented. When you execute like this, you're still behind the airplane. The machine is still flying you.

FROM FRAGMENTATION TO FLOW

At some point, with enough practice, you enter another phase. You move beyond the fragmentation of specific steps, and each aerobatic maneuver becomes a single motion. You no longer think in terms of sequences. Now it's one evolution, one maneuver, one landing. Everything becomes more fluid, and while there are still steps in your mind, they are much larger. They contain all of those little pieces in a single space. Barrel roll becomes one motion, instead of many, and your string of conscious decisions becomes a set of maneuvers, instead of countless small steps. You lose a sense of the pieces that make up each. When you reach this point, you're no longer behind the jet, you're ahead. Your thinking moves from the present, and you start to create the future. The shift is both mental and physical.

This is the phase where I believe most pilots—or if we're talking in more general terms, most high performers—ultimately end up. But for me, once the flight hours racked up, I began to feel a development that took me even further. After thousands of hours of flight, my perspective changed. It was a kind of mental expansion, a highly focused awareness. It's neither ahead nor behind, but rather it's a feeling of extreme presence. It was an awareness of connectedness, not only to my task, but also to the world around me. The duality of man and machine faded, and the jet became like an extension of my body. I was no longer thinking about the mechanical components, or the objects in the cockpit around me. I wasn't flying a jet. I was simply flying. My motions became instinctual, natural, and along with that new awareness, my mastery of the task greatly increased. Elite athletes come to this same experience.

The amazing thing is, the feeling of connectedness didn't stop with me. Later on, when I was flying with the Blue Angels, I eventually felt it extend beyond my canopy and encompass all the other jets and pilots around me in the formation. At first, when a new team comes together, you feel like six separate individuals. That's the challenge with putting a new team together; you have to make six individuals grow and expand until you become one team, one formation. It only happens over time. The more we flew together, the more we grew accustomed to one another. Through countless briefs and debriefs, my experience of connectedness began to expand beyond myself. Slowly, I began to feel an expansion that encompassed the other pilots and the jets around me. Flying in formation, for us, became as natural as a flock of birds (granted, a flock moving at 500 mph!).

BEYOND HIGH PERFORMANCE

This is the state *beyond high performance* that I wish for every individual and team that I work with. In this state, there is an undeniable chemistry. There is a bond that holds us together. On the Blues, that connection allows us to go tearing through the sky as a single entity. On any team, borders begin to dissolve. We become more like nature: when one of us moves, all of us instinctively react. It's not a simple matter of verbal communication or sequential thinking. At this point, we are beyond all of that. It becomes a flow. It becomes a team.

Once you've had this experience of oneness, it's always available to you. Once you know what it feels like, you keep working toward creating the conditions—internally and externally—that allow it to happen over and over again. The more often it happens, the more often it will keep happening. The brain reconditions itself through repetition. Again, Hebb's rule: "Neurons that fire together, wire together."

Achieving this state of connectedness is a signal that you are beginning to move beyond high performance. This moment doesn't come from just working harder. It's more like a shift on the inside and the outside. It comes from consistency and deliberate actions; and it manifests as joyful effort. That's exactly what the combination of process and mindset gives you. It breaks down performance into small components that are easy to tackle. It's going to take effort to get where you want to go, but when you can break things down, building upward becomes natural.

Hebb's rule: "Neurons that fire together, wire together.

When you get into that flow, you gain something incredible: a sense of peace that flows from both power and grace. There is a natural thrill to seeing ourselves improve, even by small degrees. As you begin to realize the benefits of organized, focused action, you approach each task with a new appreciation. Every cycle represents an opportunity for growth and learning. The pace of joyful effort is different. It has internal power with the grace of humility. It's authority, but with kindness, a calming strength. You understand that at times it will be difficult to face challenges and obstacles, but because of your awareness, you have confidence and faith.

If you're struggling with a challenge, joyful effort might sound hard to obtain. So how do you ground yourself in this mindset? How can you find a way to work with joyful effort, no matter what you're doing? There are triggers we can all use, like the Glad To Be Here Wake-Up.

But I employ another trigger in my life every day. I like to call it an "I am . . . " statement. It's a manifestation of a powerful personal CenterPoint. What you put after "I am . . . " is important and can affect how you do everything. Creating this statement is universally applicable because I believe all of us have passion within that is waiting to be ignited. We simply need to unleash it.

What you put after "I am . . . " is important and can affect how you do everything.

Here's something I say to myself every day: "I am an angel." That may sound a little bold, but I don't use it as a boast. This is my statement because it's a way to put myself in service of others. The word *angel* brings emotion and power to me because it is related to my past—on some level it's true, I was a *Blue* Angel—and it stirs deep emotions in me. It gives me the feeling I'm activating a core life force. Some years ago I was doing some research. I read that there are five qualities that define an angel. An angel is a **messenger**. An angel gives **guidance**. An angel **protects**. An angel is a **warrior**. And above all else, an angel **serves others**. I'm not sure these are the only qualities of an angel, but I said to myself, "If that's it, I'm in."

Those are the same qualities that I try to bring with me as I work with individuals and teams around the world to reach their highest potential. That statement has taken me to a lot of interesting places over the years. As it drives my actions, it inspires me to continue down a path of continuous growth. It inspires me to embrace the very system that I'm sharing with you, and it reminds me of the importance to go beyond and see the world at a deeper level.

Formerly as a Blue and even in my current role, I've had the privilege to impact hundreds of thousands of people. But you don't have to be on a stage to create an impact; we all have this ability to serve others. There is something about giving and sharing that is essential for going beyond. When we are generous, it expands our understanding of the world beyond our current task and beyond ourselves. The effects are positive in ways that surpass our initial ability to comprehend them. I want to tell a quick story that demonstrates how we often have no idea of the effect we'll have on someone's life. In the same way, we often have no idea of the effect we can have on the world at large.

The Blue Angels enthusiastically embrace the wisdom of their ex-members, and I frequently have the opportunity to go back and work with the team. This year, I first connected with them early in the show season. The team was preparing for an air show in Idaho Falls, a short drive from my home in Sun Valley. I arrived at the base and made my usual rounds, trying to make myself available to everyone. First, I instinctively drove to where the maintenance troops were working on the jets. I asked them about the aircraft and how the show season was going. We got personal and talked about their travels, how they had been spending their time. On the flight line, I had a chance to really connect with them and tell them what a great job they were doing. My next stop was the com-cart, where I spoke with the show narrator (#7) and the maintenance officer. I love experiencing the subtleties of each new team. There's a camaraderie that extends well beyond the current members. I watched the demo pilots taxi out the jets. I can remember what it felt like to be in that cockpit. I hadn't met all of these pilots yet, but I knew what was going on in their heads at this moment—excitement and challenge at the same time.

As I stood on the tarmac and watched the practice show, I realized that to this day, even after I know what it's like on the inside of the air show, I still stand in awe of the flying, just like I did as a little boy at my first air show.

After the flight, I went into the debrief with the team. In these situations, I'm there to support them in their current methodology. Normally, former team members sit around the outside of the room with the maintenance officer and other support officers. But this time they pulled me up to the table and asked me to participate directly in the debrief. I sat between the two solo pilots, #5 and #6. The motions, cadence, and standards were similar to how they had been when I flew with the team, more than 20 years ago. As the debrief progressed, things opened up a bit, and they started asking me some questions about my experience. Specifically, they wanted to know about the Section High Alpha, the maneuver I helped create when I was on the team.

When I told them about how we initially did a split-S off the line-abreast loop, and made a vertical rendezvous, they couldn't believe we'd attempted that. Of course, we didn't do it that way for long; it only took a few attempts before we realized we needed to change, for safety reasons, to a horizontal rendezvous. That's what I included when I wrote the standard operating procedure, which is still in the Blue Angel manual today. The next day #6 came up to me and said, "Gucci, all I've been thinking about the last 24 hours is that vertical split-S rendezvous, 200 feet off the deck!" It's impressive to see how certain traditions and standards of bearing last, but it's so fun to share the differences too.

At the end of the debrief, everyone was getting ready to depart and I was approached by #3, one of the brand-new pilots. His name was Nate, but I hadn't had a chance to talk to him yet. He put his arm around me and said, "Gucci, it's great to see you again." I said it was great to meet him, all the while wondering why he thought we'd already met. He said, "No, you don't understand. Let me show you something." That's when he handed me his phone with a picture on its screen: it was me as #7, kneeling with a little boy on my knee. I realized he was right, we had met before!

"That was when I was five years old," he said, "and since then, I kept this picture above my bed, along with a picture of the whole team flying. I did that my entire life, going through high school, college, and even in the military." He could tell I was blown away. Then he added, "It's amazing, dreams do come true!"

That was the moment I realized how important every inter-action can be. I didn't remember sharing that moment with Nate, or the countless thousands with other kids, but he sure did. It goes to show, you never know the impact you can have with simple generosity. Thirty seconds can change a life.

We all have those opportunities; if we are present and living in our abundant nature, we start to see them. I thought back to my conversation with Captain Rud at the Pentagon, when I phoned to ask for the F-18 orders. It was the same situation: a small, forgettable piece of his time translated into a life-altering event for me. Most of the time, you never know if you made an impact—but with Nate, I got to see the full circle. The cool part is, we all have this opportunity. These are the kinds of opportunities you see when you move beyond yourself and into the abundant mindset. It's a matter of being present and remaining aware; that's what allows us to have a positive impact on the world.

After that encounter with Nate, where I was frankly blown away, we kept in touch. Eventually, I was with the Blues again at the end of the season, when they have a celebration in which there is a formal transition of the team. The people who are leaving are recognized, and introduced one last time as "Blue Angels, 2017." At that point the energy of the room shifts, and they introduce for the first time the new team as the "Blue Angels, 2018." Nate was transitioning from #3 to #4, about to become a slot pilot, a second-year Blue and mentor to the incoming pilots.

After the formalities, he grabbed me and said, "I want to introduce you to my parents." It reminded me of when I was on the team, how the families become part of the extended Blue Angel family. They were so proud of him, and it reinforced how that moment at the air show impacted his entire life. His wife even told me that the picture still hangs in their living room. I couldn't believe it.

Then we had a moment to speak one-on-one. I congratulated Nate on his new leadership role. The interesting thing is, when he had my ear, he wasn't interested in hearing cool stories or talking about flying. The main thing he wanted to talk about was how to have a greater impact. Specifically, he wanted to discuss presenting to and inspiring kids. I love that he asked me about this, because that was my passion when I was on the Blues. Every Friday morning you get to share your story by going to schools and giving them a glimpse into the awe of flying. For me, speaking to youth is amazing because each child is so full of hope.

Nate and I spent 20 minutes talking about how to give an impactful presentation, how to reach people in an audience, whoever they might be. Being successful speaking to kids is about the same as speaking to CEOs or anyone else. You have to connect in an authentic way. You have to make your story relevant to them. Otherwise it's just a cool story. We need to be able to recognize that every person has unique gifts, dreams, and challenges. I use my own story of wanting to become a Blue Angel when I was a child. I tell the children, "I wasn't different than you; look what's possible when you put your mind to it and believe."

As I was telling Nate this, I realized that he and I shared something specific. He was in the exact same position to tell that story, and light a spark in the eyes of these children. It's amazing to know that someone I impacted in a way I didn't realize would become at once the fulfillment of his dreams, and the source of inspiration for another generation.

Along with this realization, I felt something very special. I felt the mindset that defines the space beyond high performance. I felt the connection between the heart and the head. I felt deeply *Glad To Be Here.*

Glad To Be Here happens to be the same feeling that inspires a process of growth, personal and professional. It is both the spark and the fuel that drives one's passion. Knowing that Nate and others were taking on this role as ambassadors and role models, I felt gratefulness for the present, the past, and the future. It's all-encompassing, and it not only gives you a certain internal peace, but also an even deeper sense of fulfillment. Glad To Be Here is the secret sauce that makes life meaningful.

In this mindset, the world lights up, and everything becomes significant. Tasks start to appear effortless. You're in a state of knowing, not just thinking. And the opposite feeling? Like you're paddling upriver!

Glad To Be Here is the secret sauce that makes life meaningful.

Glad To Be Here feels like you're in the flow of the river; yes, there are adjustments to make, but you're naturally moving forward. The gratitude mindset puts you in a state where you're not only open to opportunities, but you actively sense them. It's something that you can activate in yourself. If you practice the Glad To Be Here mindset, it can change your perspective and change your life.

Can you imagine how you'd feel if you saw that same perspective reflected in everyone around you?

PLANTING SEEDS

There's something I've learned about gratitude over the years: when you feel it, all you want to do is share it. You have a deep desire to spread this feeling. It activates a sense of generosity and a desire to give to others around you. And second, gratitude is contagious. When one person shares it, it changes the perspective of people around them, who in turn want to share that special emotion with others.

The way that gratitude affects others has shaped one of my deeply held beliefs. It's the one that defines all of my actions, and it's the reason I wrote this book. *I believe that Glad To Be Here has the power to change the entire world.*

The Glad To Be Here mindset is a deep state of joy. It's a state of abundance. It's generosity imbued with gratitude. It's inspiration and passion, with honor and integrity. It's power with grace. It's joy with hope, faith, and love. It's authenticity and presence. It's kindness with wisdom. And above all, it's oneness: peace and prosperity.

I believe each of us wields a small piece of the greater power that can make this world a better place for everyone. This is a power that is inherent in each of us. The change starts small, but remember: gratitude is contagious. At the highest level, I believe there is an extreme power here, and it all starts with you. So, as Gandhi said: be the change you want to see in the world.

In the space between thought and action, you find life.

In the space between thought and action, you find life. In these moments, you become your choices. You become what you think and what you surround yourself with. Your awareness of this space creates your destiny. Through your actions, you are affecting countless story lines of everyone around you. When you imbue excellence with Glad To Be Here, you have an operating system that allows you to see things others don't see and gives you the confidence to take action. These are the kinds of opportunities you see when you take on the Glad To Be Here mindset.

When you imbue excellence with Glad To Be Here, you have an operating system that allows you to see things others don't see and gives you the confidence to take action.

This is my challenge to you: Go Beyond. Use the wisdom and knowledge in this book to seize the day, be your best, and create positive change in your life. Use your passion as a launching pad to take yourself into rare air. What I find most inspiring is the knowledge that every single day, in every moment, in every interaction, we have the opportunity to make a difference. That fact has the power to change our lives and change the world. It all comes down to a simple phrase: **Glad To Be Here.**

Go Beyond.

Look beyond the horizon.

Look beyond that horizon.

That is where Awesome lives.

Glad To Be Here.

Acknowledgments

I want to extend my deepest thanks and feelings of Glad To Be Here to everyone who made this book possible.

First and foremost, to my writing partner, Matthew Sanders, who brought this book to life and helped tell my story in a meaningful way—I couldn't have done this without you! To my entire family: my wife Carol, who is my love, inspiration, and foundation; my dad for being the embodiment of wisdom and compassion; my mom for showing me the meaning of love and kindness; and my sister for being fearless and offering her unwavering support over the course of our lives. To all Blue Angels, past, present, and future; I feel like I'm standing on the shoulders of giants. To Greg "Boss" Wooldridge and Mike "Wizzard" McCabe for being my core mentors today and continuing this amazing journey with me. To Michael Roach, for years of inspiration, guidance, and friendship. To Patrick Cowden of Beyond Leadership, for being there when I needed to stoke the flames. To Mike Barlow, Ben Ortlip, and Brent Cole, who have made a deep impression on this book. To the entire team at John Foley Inc., who keep everything moving in the background, every single day. And finally, to everyone I've had the opportunity to work with, to inspire, and to be inspired by.

Glad To Be Here!

About John Foley
CenterPoint Companies, Inc.

We believe that transcendent potential for greatness lives within every individual, every team, and every organization. That is why we founded John Foley Center Point Companies, to create inspirational experiences and dynamic programs that transform organizations and people's lives.

- ◆ Keynotes, Workshops, Online Curriculum

- ◆ Individuals, Teams, Organizations

- ◆ High Performance, Leadership, Teamwork

- ◆ Trust, Beliefs, Alignment, Culture, Gratitude

- ◆ Impacting over 1,000 organizations and 500,000 people

Learn more on how John Foley Inc. can help transform you and your team.

www.johnfoleyinc.com   info@johnfoleyinc.com

The Glad To Be Here Foundation

Throughout my career, I always felt it was important to express my gratitude by giving back. In 2011, we founded the Glad To Be Here Foundation as a way to make a positive difference in the world. Through the foundation, we donate 10 percent of our proceeds to charity.

My wife Carol and I have donated more than $1.8 million to over 347 charities in 57 countries and sponsor 47 children worldwide. Our goal is to sponsor a child in every country; we believe more Fearless giving is needed to create positive change in the world.

We have contributed to hundreds of diverse charities: Doctors Without Borders, Senior Connection, Homes For Our Troops, Make A Wish, Ronald McDonald House, American Heart Association, Himalayan Cataract Project, Cystic Fibrosis Foundation, Best Friends Animal Sanctuary, St. Jude's Children's Research Hospital, Guide Dogs for the Blind, Habitat for Humanity, The Hunger Coalition, NAMI and Plan International are only a few.

The Glad To Be Here mindset is a deep state of joy. It is a state of abundance. It is generosity imbued with gratitude. It is inspiration and passion with honor and integrity.

The Glad To Be Here mindset is not passive; it is an attitude that grows deeper with every act of kindness and charity.

Glad To Be Here!

www.gladtobeherefoundation.org

About the Author

JOHN FOLEY is a former lead solo pilot of the Blue Angels, Sloan Fellow at Stanford's Graduate School of Business, entrepreneur, venture capitalist, leadership expert, speaker, and Gratitude Guru. As a thought leader on high performance, John created the "Glad To Be Here" Mindset Methodology and the Diamond Performance Framework. These programs inspire individuals, teams and organizations around the world to reach their highest potential.

John graduated from the US Naval Academy with a BS in Mechanical Engineering and was a defensive back for the Midshipmen. He was chosen as "Top Ten Carrier Pilot" six times before becoming an F/A-18 Instructor Pilot.

He holds three master's degrees: MA in National Security & Strategic Studies from the Naval War College; Stanford MS in Management, as a Sloan fellow from Stanford Graduate School of Business; and MA in International Policy Studies from Stanford University. John was also a Fellow at Stanford Center on International Conflict and Negotiation and was awarded an honorary PhD from UNAM, Universidad Nacional Autónoma de México.

For decades, John has shared his exciting, rare journey with audiences around the world, becoming one of the most in-demand leadership and performance experts. John has spoken on 5 continents, 20 countries and over 1,000 events working with some of the world's top organizations such as; Google, Intel, Cisco, Microsoft, HP, Mercedes Benz, BMW, IBM, Hitachi, Chevron, BP, Marriott, Hilton, Penske Racing, Alabama Football, LA Kings, Merrill Lynch, Morgan Stanley, Edward Jones, Fidelity, Mass Mutual, MetLife, Bank of America, Deloitte, IBM, Hershey, P&G, Philips, Etihad, America Hospital Association, Blue Cross, and the Mayo Clinic. He has also been a featured speaker at NBA, MLB, MLS, NCAA, TEDx, VC and CEO summits, Titan Summit, USNA Leadership Conference, and Stanford Business School.